THE TOP 15

NOVA SCOTIA'S GREATEST ATHLETES

NOVA SCOTIA SPORT HALL OF FAME

PROCEEDS SUPPORT
The Nova Scotia Sport Hall of Fame &
The Tim Horton Children's Foundation

NOVA SCOTIA
Sport Hall of Fame

NIMBUS
PUBLISHING
— NIMBUS.CA —

Nimbus Publishing Limited
3660 Strawberry Hill Street, Halifax, NS, B3K 5A9
(902) 455-4286 nimbus.ca

Printed and bound in Canada

NB1399

Cover & interior design: John van der Woude, JVDW Designs

Library and Archives Canada Cataloguing in Publication

The top 15 : Nova Scotia's greatest athletes / Nova Scotia
Sport Hall of Fame.

ISBN 978-1-77108-701-8 (softcover)

1. Athletes--Nova Scotia—Biography. 2. Sports—Nova Scotia—History. I.
Nova Scotia Sport Hall of Fame, issuing body II. Title: Top fifteen.

GV697.A1T66 2018   796.092'2716   C2018-902932-3

Nimbus Publishing acknowledges the financial support for its publishing activities from the Government of Canada through the Canada Book Fund (CBF) and the Canada Council for the Arts, and from the Province of Nova Scotia. We are pleased to work in partnership with the Province of Nova Scotia to develop and promote our creative industries for the benefit of all Nova Scotians.

Sept. 24, 2018

FOREWORD

by Bruce Rainnie

To Don,
A great producer! an even better friend Thanks for the guidance, laughs and support!
Your friend always...
Bruce

If you love sports, then I bet you are generally keen to engage in a good argument. For example, if you're a hockey fan, you've likely at one time gone toe-to-toe with someone over this question: "Who is the greatest NHL player of all time?"

Now, in my opinion, the three best NHL players ever are, in order—Bobby Orr, Mario Lemieux, and Wayne Gretzky. (Sidney Crosby is getting closer to this top three with each year that passes.) When I share this with many of my hockey buddies, though, inevitably I am told that I have Gretzky ranked too low, that he was better than either Lemieux or Orr. As a proponent of good debate, I always welcome these comments and am happy to defend my choices. As sports fans, it's what many of us like to do.

It was in this spirit that we at the Nova Scotia Sport Hall of Fame decided to embark on a project to list the "Top 15" Nova Scotia athletes of all time. It seemed timely, given that 2017 marked the 150th anniversary of Canada's Confederation, and fifteen is a natural numerical derivative of 150. We knew it would engender discussion and controversy, but we also knew it would get people talking about a collection of athletes that would be the envy of any province in the country.

We started with a list of one hundred and two athletes and enlisted a committee of twenty-four people (current and former athletes, current and former coaches, current and former members of the Nova Scotia sports media, current and former sport builders) to whittle this down to twenty-five.

We then asked *another* committee of twelve to sit in a room for three hours on a hot July afternoon and rank the Top 15. Votes from the public factored in as well and counted collectively as the thirteenth committee member. We urged our committee to rank based on the following nine criteria:

1. **Dominance:** How big was/is the athlete's gap over their peers?
2. **Achievement**: Did the athlete have Olympic medals, World championships, World records, Pan Am medals, National championships, Stanley Cups, Grey Cups, and major awards?
3. **Consistency**: Can/could the athlete be counted on to consistently deliver great performances?
4. **Longevity**: For how long was the athlete great?
5. **Skill Range**: Can you imagine the athlete being great at many sports?
6. **Wow Factor**: When you watch the athlete perform, can he/she do things that most others simply can't?
7. **Depth/Quality of Competition**: How good are/were the opponents?
8. **Performance Under Pressure**: In the biggest moments, how good is/was the athlete?
9. **Legacy**: To what degree can you think of the sport in Nova Scotia without thinking of this athlete?

That's how we did it. Was our process perfect? Probably not. But it was as thorough and transparent as we could make it and it has unearthed a list that is simply sensational. I can guarantee it will stand the test of time and is a reflection of just how great Nova Scotia athletes have been and continue to be. As a relatively small province, we have always punched way above our weight.

A special thanks to CBC Nova Scotia and the *Halifax Chronicle Herald* for partnering with us as we unveiled the Top 15 Athletes in the fall of 2017. Their contributions helped to generate an interest and momentum that was admittedly surprising, but certainly welcomed.

Special thanks as well to Top 15 chairman Joel Jacobson, vice-chair Gordie Sutherland, and Hall of Fame staff members Katie Tanner, Shane Mailman, Christina Brien, and Karolyn Sevcik. Each went above and beyond to make this idea a reality.

This book is the result not only of the efforts of those mentioned above, but also of a wonderful partnership between the Nova Scotia Sport Hall of Fame and Tim Hortons store owners in Nova Scotia. They have supported this project with tremendous enthusiasm from the very outset. I am proud to say that all proceeds from the sale of the book will be split between the Hall and the Tim Horton Children's Foundation.

So all that's left now is for you to sit back, relax, turn the pages, and enjoy. And as you do, always remember that Orr was better than Gretzky.

Or was he?

THE
TOP 15
NOVA SCOTIA'S
GREATEST
ATHLETES
NOVA SCOTIA
SPORT HALL
OF FAME

ROB McCALL

...outh, Ice Dancing, Inducted 1993

By Greg Guy, with introduction by Katie Tanner

Rob McCall's name is mentioned so often in Nova Scotia sport circles that you would think the champion ice dancer was still dazzling audiences with his footwork and flair. While this talented athlete may no longer be with us, the brightness of both his accomplishments and personality have kept the memory of McCall from fading.

Nova Scotians who remember the local figure-skating frenzy that he and partner Marie McNeil inspired in the 1970s will tell you that McCall was destined for greatness. Other athletes from the province—such as boxer Ricky Anderson, who met McCall at the Canada Games when they were both starting out in their athletic careers—will tell you that McCall was a genuinely kind and generous person.

McCall's friends and acquaintances throughout Halifax and further abroad will tell you every detail they remember about the skater, from his Halifax Skating Club days to the significance of his Olympic bronze medal—the one that made him and partner Tracy Wilson the first Canadian ice dancers to make it onto the Olympic podium.

The article reprinted below was written by Greg Guy for McCall's posthumous induction to the Hall of Fame in 1993 and it accurately describes the lasting effect that McCall has had on skating in Canada:

A solitary spotlight shone at centre ice in a darkened Varsity Arena in Toronto on November 21, 1992. Surrounding the light were twenty-six of the world's best figure skaters, each with their right arm stretched toward the tiny circle of light. It was a symbol, an effective one—a tribute to a friend. It symbolized Robert David McCall's presence and spirit, as his skating friends and family carried out one of his final wishes to have a benefit skating show to raise funds for HIV-AIDS research.

On November 15, 1991, the skating community was saddened with the loss of McCall to AIDS-related cancer. Not only did a superb athlete leave us that Friday afternoon—also gone was a budding innovator and artist with a vibrant personality, who had the ability to make the world cheer and laugh, on and off the ice, with his outrageous sense of humour.

His good friend and fellow Olympic teammate Brian Orser said McCall was philosophical about his illness: "He said he'd lived more in thirty-two years than most people live in a lifetime."

In his twenty-one years of competitive skating, he rose to stardom in the skating world, winning Canada's first-ever Olympic ice-dance bronze medal with partner Tracy Wilson at the 1988 Winter Games in Calgary, and in one of their final competitions, becoming World

DID YOU KNOW?

- McCall was the first Nova Scotian to bring home a medal from the Winter Olympics.

- McCall and McNeil's success as National champions in 1981 is credited with influencing the decision to have Halifax host the 1990 World Figure Skating Championships at the (then) Metro Centre.

- CBC put McCall and Wilson on their 2017 list of the Top 10 Canadian Figure Skating Champions, stating that they "show[ed] the world that ice dance wasn't only a European thing."

- As a child, McCall would accompany his mother to the Dartmouth Rink where she taught figure skating and power skating.

professional champions in 1989 at Landover, Maryland.

McCall began his skating career in Halifax-Dartmouth and was first known on the national skating scene with Halifax partner Marie McNeil. McCall and McNeil formed their partnership in 1972, and by the late 1970s the duo became a household name in Nova Scotia. In their first international competition at the 1977 World Junior Figure Skating Championships at Megève, France, they placed a remarkable third. They also won the Canadian junior title the same year. Waltzing into the senior ranks in 1978, McCall and McNeil danced steadily to the top of the podium, skating to bronze medals in 1978 and 1979, finishing second in 1980, and finally winning their first Canadian senior title on home ice at the Halifax Metro Centre in 1981.

In 1982, Dartmouth's McCall teamed up with Port Moody, BC's, Wilson. When East met West the new tandem was unstoppable. They danced cheek to cheek as National senior champs for seven consecutive years. In their World Championships debut in 1982 in Copenhagen, Wilson and McCall placed tenth. In 1983 in Helsinki and 1984 in Ottawa, they were sixth at the Worlds. There were eighth at the 1984 Olympic Games in Sarajevo, Yugoslavia. In 1985, following the retirement of Olympic champions Jayne Torvill and Christopher Dean of Britain, Wilson and McCall worked their way up to fourth at the Worlds in Tokyo.

In the next three Worlds at Geneva (1986), Cincinnati (1987), and Budapest (1988), they won bronze medals. McCall once told his mother, Evelyn, "Don't worry, Mom, it's okay. Bronze is only a darker shade of gold."

In April 1988, [after winning Olympic bronze], Wilson and McCall turned professional. [Following their World Professional Championships win], Wilson went on to television broadcasting and McCall, always the innovator, turned his attention to choreography. He designed his own programs as well as those for skaters like Orser and world champ Kurt Browning.

Today, Evelyn, McCall's brother Steve, skaters, and friends continue to skate McCall's dream. They have established a foundation in his name to help promote AIDS awareness, education, and research, and, hopefully, one day achieve Rob's ultimate goal—to find a cure.

Rob McCall may have left the world too soon, but his spirit, determination, and dreams live on. Skaters and skating audiences everywhere will never forget McCall "the entertainer" and his contributions to the sport of figure skating.

TAKE THEIR WORD FOR IT

"What is unique about figure skating is that, in addition to being a sport, it is also artistic as well as a form of entertainment. What made Rob a unique champion in our sport is he had it all. He was an outstanding athlete, a true artist, and a one-of-a-kind showman."

—Marie (McNeil) Bowness, Hall of Famer and McCall's former skating partner

15 MEMORABLE MOMENTS IN NOVA SCOTIA SPORT

1 **1873**: George Brown, the fisherman from Herring Cove, beats out international rowers at the Halifax Aquatic Carnival to become the fastest single sculler in the world in the five-mile race.

2 **1891**: Three Nova Scotians (Finlay MacDonald, John Thompson, and Lyman Archibald) play in the very first basketball game, which was organized by Dr. James Naismith in Springfield, Massachusetts.

3 **1919**: His Royal Highness the Prince of Wales visits the Studley Quoit Club in Halifax.

4 **1935**: After winning the Maritime Senior Baseball Championships, the Yarmouth Gateways play the Boston Braves in an exhibition game in Yarmouth. Although the Braves defeat the Gateways, this is the first time a major league team visits Nova Scotia.

5 **1942**: Babe Ruth visits Halifax's Wanderers Grounds for the Navy League opening day and gives a batting exhibition.

6 **1950**: Nova Scotians first hear Danny Gallivan as the voice of the Montreal Canadiens when he is asked to fill in for Doug Smith on New Year's Eve.

7 **1951**: Don Oyler's Glooscap curling rink from Kentville goes undefeated to win the Brier on Halifax ice.

8 **1964**: Boxer Delmore "Buddy" Daye defeats Jackie "Kid" Carter to win the Canadian super featherweight championship at the Halifax Forum.

9 **1969**: The first Canada Summer Games are held in Halifax/Dartmouth.

10 **1972**: In their inaugural season, the Nova Scotia Voyageurs become the first Canada-based hockey team to win the Calder Cup with their championship game on home ice.

11 **1978**: Saint Mary's defeats Acadia in a CIS basketball showdown for the National championship in front of 11,000 spectators at the Halifax Metro Centre.

12 **1979**: Nova Scotians Clyde Gray and Chris Clarke face off in a boxing match at the Metro Centre, with Clarke winning the British Commonwealth welterweight title in front of 10,000 fans.

13 **1981**: Rob McCall and Marie (McNeil) Bowness win the Canadian ice dancing pairs championship at the Metro Centre, raising Nova Scotia's figure-skating profile.

14 **1988**: Golfer Gordie Smith places seventh at the Canadian Open ahead of legends Jack Nicklaus and Greg Norman.

15 **2003**: Halifax and Sydney host the World Junior Hockey Championships, where Canada plays Russia in the finals. Russia goes on to defeat Canada, but the event puts Nova Scotia on the map as a premium sport event destination.

MARK DE JONGE

Halifax, Sprint Kayak
By Bruce Rainnie

In the beginning, the goal for Mark de Jonge was very simple—don't fall in!

"I was thirteen when I first learned about paddling. My parents enrolled me in the Maskwa Aquatic Club, really as a way to meet other kids. My first days were spent holding onto the dock and trying my very best not to tip over. But every day, I got further and further away from the dock. And by the fall, I was starting to really like the speed I could hit in a kayak."

De Jonge took the sport seriously from day one, and he became very good very quickly. In 1998, just a year into the sport, he finished second at the bantam championships held in Nova Scotia and qualified for the midget age group at Nationals, although he did not end up travelling to Whistler, BC, to compete. A year later, he qualified again and actually won the K1 1,000-metre event. But from there, his path to stardom was anything but silky smooth.

"I was racing the 500-metre and 1,000-metre events and was doing pretty well. But even though I was always in the hunt, these distances were always tough for me. I always felt like I was swimming upstream and I really struggled with the training."

De Jonge failed to qualify for the 2004 Olympics in Athens and the 2008 Olympics in Beijing. Discouraged, he took some time away from the sport and wasn't sure he would ever return. But then fate intervened. In 2009, the International Olympic Committee announced that the 200-metre K1 race would be an Olympic event.

"I had been really questioning my future in the sport. Looking back now, I realize that my zest for paddling was basically gone," remembers de Jonge. "But then my passion for the sport was fully renewed when I realized that this new event was just tailor-made for me."

Scott Logan, Canoe Kayak Canada's former high-performance coach, explains why the marriage between de Jonge and the 200-metre sprint was so seamless: "Mark is so powerful and has such wonderful reaction time and fast-twitch muscles. His explosion off the start line is exceptional, really among the best I've ever seen. So physically, he couldn't be more suited for this distance. And mentally? Well, one of his favourite sports is Formula One racing. So he loves speed, and he loves to leave you in the dust."

Success came very quickly for de Jonge at this new distance. He won his first World Cup medal in 2011 and then a year later, at the London Olympics, he fought through a painful hand injury to win bronze. He had officially served notice to the paddling world that he had returned, with a renewed enthusiasm and focus.

In 2013, he won silver at the ICF Canoe Sprint World Championships. But his best would come a year later when the Worlds were held in Moscow.

"If you want to have any success at this distance, you have to be flawless for about thirty-four seconds. One little mistake and you can

TAKE THEIR WORD FOR IT

Mark de Jonge and I have been friends, opponents, and teammates for over twenty years. He's always been one of the most positive guys to be on the water with, on a long flight with, or in the back of the boathouse with. He's demonstrated first-hand how resilience and determination produce a world champion. Mark wasn't an overnight gold medallist; he didn't win until he had been competing on the world scene for over a decade. He didn't qualify for the first Olympics he tried out for or the second. He stuck with it and believed in himself and continues to inspire young Canadian paddlers to do the same.

—Adam van Koeverden, Olympic K1 gold, silver, and bronze medallist go from first to eighth in a blink. In 2014 in Moscow, the stars really aligned," recalls de Jonge.

So much so that de Jonge set a world record (33.945) in the semi-final and went on to win gold with a time of 33.961. The paddler from the Maskwa Aquatic Club had reached the summit of his sport, and his years of training at various distances had paid off on the grandest stage.

"As a sprinter, you have to be powerful, but you also have to have a good deal of endurance. It's only a 200-metre race, but the last 50 metres you're basically burning up and trying to keep everything together. So it's a combination of probably my past in the 1,000 and having that endurance base built up over the years, and just knowing how to fight through pain. That never-give-up attitude has allowed me to tough it out over those last 50 metres."

In 2015, de Jonge rode that attitude to a gold medal at the Pan Am Games in Toronto and another World Championships gold

DID YOU KNOW?

- De Jonge applies physics and math to his training, studying how to use energy to give himself a competitive advantage.

- De Jonge graduated from Dalhousie University in 2009 with a degree in civil engineering.

- De Jonge's favourite quotation is from former Texas A&M football coach Homer Norton: "It's how you show up to the showdown that counts."

medal, this one in Milan, Italy. He was a heavy favourite heading into the 2016 Summer Olympics in Rio, but finished a disappointing seventh out of eight boats in the final. Following the race, he admitted that he had perhaps done too much thinking and not enough paddling in preparation for the event.

"Maybe overanalyzing and really breaking things down stroke by stroke. I think when you focus too much on that you take away some of the emotion of just going out and crushing it," says de Jonge. "That's what I wanted to do that day; I just got to the line saying, 'You're just going to floor it the whole way; stop thinking, your body knows what to do.' I did that, but I just didn't have it that day, unfortunately."

After the 2016 Olympics, de Jonge again took some time away from the sport. He needed a break from the water and a chance to "recharge some batteries that were testing pretty low." During that time, he and his wife became parents to a little boy named Maxim. He also seriously contemplated retirement. However, after lengthy reflection, he decided there would be at least one more chapter.

"My plan is to return in 2018, with an eye toward the 2020 Summer Olympics in Tokyo. Four years between Games seems like an eternity. But the time from 2012 to 2016 really flew by. It actually felt like no time had passed. My love for the sport is back, and when you have that to drive you, everything seems a bit more manageable. I think I have one more great run in me, one that I hope culminates with my best performance in the summer of 2020."

THE FIRST 15 NOVA SCOTIAN OLYMPIANS

1 **Ronald J. MacDonald**: track and field (marathon), Paris, 1900 (competed for the United States). Won the second-ever Boston Marathon (1898).

2 **Simon P. Gillis**: hammer throw, St. Louis, London, and Stockholm, 1904, 1908, and 1912 (competed for the United States; couldn't compete in 1912 due to injury). Set the world record for hammer throw twice and once single-handedly defeated six men in tug-of-war.

3 **Garfield MacDonald**: track and field (hop-step-jump), London, 1908 (won silver). Also competed in high jump, broad jump, pole vault, tennis, and golf.

4 **Duncan Gillis**: hammer throw, Stockholm, 1912 (won silver). Also won the Canadian amateur heavyweight wrestling title in 1913.

5 **Victor MacAulay**: track and field (marathon), Paris, 1924. Won the *Halifax Herald* Modified Marathon five times and finished in the top ten at the Boston Marathon four times.

6 **Silas McLellan**: track and field (marathon), Amsterdam, 1928. Won the *Halifax Herald* Modified Marathon five times and the *Herald* full marathon twice.

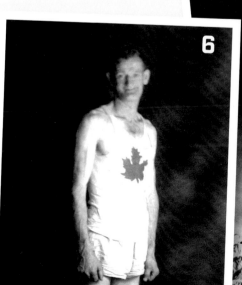

7 **Rena MacDonald**: track and field (discus), Amsterdam, 1928 (competed for the United States). Was US National Championship winner in women's discus for 1929 and US National Championship winner for women's shot put in 1929 and 1930.

8 **Johnny Miles**: track and field (marathon), Amsterdam and Los Angeles, 1928 and 1932. Won the Boston Marathon twice.

9 **Aileen Meagher**: track and field, Los Angeles and Berlin, 1932 (couldn't compete due to injury) and 1936 (won bronze). Was four-time medallist at the British Empire Games.

10 **Joseph Haley**: track and field (high jump), Berlin, 1936. Held the Canadian high jump record and won silver for high jump at the 1934 British Empire Games.

11 **Les Mason**: boxing, Melbourne, 1956. Later became a long-time boxing coach and official.

12 **Garfield "Gary" McMahon**: shooting, Rome and Tokyo, 1960 and 1964. Was three-time Canadian Open champion and seven-time Pan American medallist.

13 **Joey Mullins**: track and field, Rome, 1960. Established a world indoor record for the 600-yard event.

14 **Douglas Rogers**: judo, Tokyo, 1964 (won silver). Was bronze medallist at the World Championships and three-time Pan American gold medallist.

15 **Robert Boucher**: speed skating and cycling, Grenoble (Winter) and Mexico City (Summer), 1968. Won gold in the men's 500-metre speed skating event at the first Canada Winter Games.

JAMIE BONE

Dartmouth, Wheelchair Sprinting, Inducted 1997

By Katie Tanner

Jamie Bone has a certain super-hero quality—one that *Halifax Chronicle Herald* cartoonist Bruce MacKinnon once perfectly captured in his depiction of Bone flying down the racetrack, Herculean arms propelling his wheelchair, while his competitors are obscured in a cloud of dust.

In 1988, on the wheelchair sprinting track in Seoul, South Korea, Bone's fellow Paralympians were left to eat his dust as Bone hurtled toward the finish line of the 400-metre race with a 100-metre lead.

The three-time Paralympic gold medallist had a slow start to sport, though, before he achieved great speeds on the racetrack.

14

Born with cerebral palsy, Bone did a bit of swimming in elementary school, but he didn't gain a competitive appetite until he joined the Nova Scotia Flying Wheels wheelchair basketball team at age fifteen. Bone admits that he was not a natural on the basketball court, but Flying Wheels is where he met Ross Sampson and was introduced to track.

Track appealed to Bone because it was an individual sport and he was motivated by the thought that he had to rely on himself.

The first time that Bone went to a track event, it was because they were doing local recruiting for disabled athletes. He took a look at the current track records and informed the coach, Doug Wilton from Ontario, that he could achieve those times. Wilton was skeptical, but soon realized Bone's potential when Bone placed third in a race using a basketball chair. It wasn't long before Bone was training with the national team in a proper racing chair.

Bone approached sprinting with a strong work ethic and plenty of determination. He is also quick to credit other athletes who inspired him—such as fellow Flying Wheels members Clary Stubbert and Walter Dann—and mentors who supported his development, including Flying Wheels coach Doug Wright, Peter Eriksson of Athletics Canada, and local coach Donna Richardson.

The Paralympics weren't always part of Bone's vision for his athletic career. His first major goal was to take on the American champion at the 1987 North American Championships. Bone did well at this event, winning silver in the 200- and 400-metre races and bronze in the 100-metre sprint. Still chasing gold, he cleaned up at the 1988 Canadian Championships, placing first in the 100-, 200-, and 400-metre events, setting a world record in the CP3 class for 400 metres (while racing in the pouring rain). He was also named Outstanding Male Athlete of the championships.

DID YOU KNOW?

- Bone's 400-metre world record (1:23.11), which he set at the Paralympics, stood for six years.

- Bone also set two Paralympic records in 1988: 20.9 seconds in the 100 metre and 41.78 in the 200 metre.

- Bone graduated from Saint Mary's University in 1989 with a degree in commerce. He was also the honorary chairman of the Metro United Way campaign that year.

- Bone's gold-medal 100-metre Paralympic race was supposed to be a semi-final, but he was informed only two minutes before starting that it would be the final.

- In his prime two years of racing (1987–1989), Bone never lost a race. He went 33-0 during that remarkable span.

After these successes, Bone figured this might be his only chance at the Paralympics, so he was determined to make it count. He took a six-month hiatus from his studies at Saint Mary's University and dedicated all his time to training.

Bone had been prepared for his 400-metre gold-medal win at Nationals because he had trained in both wet and windy conditions at the Saint Mary's track. He had practised adaptability, wheeling across Astroturf and even sprinting up Citadel Hill at the suggestion of Coach Richardson.

Bone started out weak in weight training, but soon Eriksson had increased Bone's weightlifting ability from 40 to 210 pounds. Bone was so obsessed with training that his parents found him wheeling around the Saint Mary's track at 10 P.M. the night before he left for Seoul. However, this was all part of his intense preparations, as he had reversed his daily schedule to be on Korean time before leaving for the Paralympics.

TAKE THEIR WORD FOR IT

Jamie had the dedication to his sport. As an elite wheelchair track star, Jamie put in countless hours of training, as you can see by his gold medals and world records. Jamie is deserving of his thirteenth spot as one of Nova Scotia's greatest athletes.

—Walter Dann, Hall of Famer, Paralympian, and Flying Wheels teammate

'BONE'-A-FIDE GOLD

Bone then had one more challenge to overcome, as he developed tendinitis right before the 1988 Paralympics. He kept his injury a secret from his competitors and relied on treatments from physiotherapist Darren Booth during the Games.

Bone describes his Paralympic experience as "surreal," especially since disabled athletics events were usually held on a local level with small crowds. The number of people at the Paralympics was overwhelming. Bone focused on maintaining his daily training routine, socializing with the support staff from Nova Scotia, and ignoring the crowds.

His focus paid off. Bone surprised himself when he won gold in the 100-metre dash after accidentally popping a wheelie at the start line. He then went on to top the podium again in the 200-metre event, even though he came to a stop at the beginning of the race when his hand slipped off his wheel. Bone's training was so superior that he was able to catch up and pass the other racers.

Finally, in the 400-metre race, Bone pushed as hard as he possibly could. He crossed the finish line and looked back in amazement as he realized there was no one behind him. He had won the race with a 100-metre lead, smashing his own world record by two full seconds.

His greatest memory from athletics is winning the 400-metre gold and hearing the Canadian anthem play as he received his medal. He also took home a bronze for the 4x100 relay event.

Bone won gold in all three individual distance events at the 1989 Canadian Championships and repeated his triple-gold at the 1989 Robin Hood Games in Nottingham, England.

He retired from competitive wheelchair sprinting at age twenty-three, already a local hero and an inspiration to many. Bone's superhuman achievements have left a lasting impression on those who followed his career in the late '80s, and his domination of the sport when it was still in its early stages of international recognition have made him a trailblazer for succeeding generations of Paralympians.

15 SPORTS AND THEIR NOVA SCOTIA PIONEERS

1 Badminton: Ken Poole of Truro, national doubles and mixed doubles champion, inducted to Nova Scotia Sport Hall of Fame, 2014.

2 Football: Wayne Smith of Halifax, Grey Cup winner, inducted 1984.

3 Golf: Graham MacIntyre of New Glasgow, represented Nova Scotia on a national level twenty-nine times, inducted 2003.

4 Harness Racing: Billy O'Donnell of Springhill, driver with over 5,700 career wins and close to $100 million in career earnings, inducted 1991.

5 Karate: Gary Sabean of Weymouth, nine-time Canadian black belt champion in the middleweight division, inducted 2010.

6 Officiating: Don Koharski of Dartmouth, official at more than 1,700 regular season National Hockey League games and close to 250 playoff games, inducted 2007.

7 Para-Athletics: Pamela LeJean of Cape Breton, Paralympian and Parapan Ams gold (shot put) and bronze (javelin) medallist.

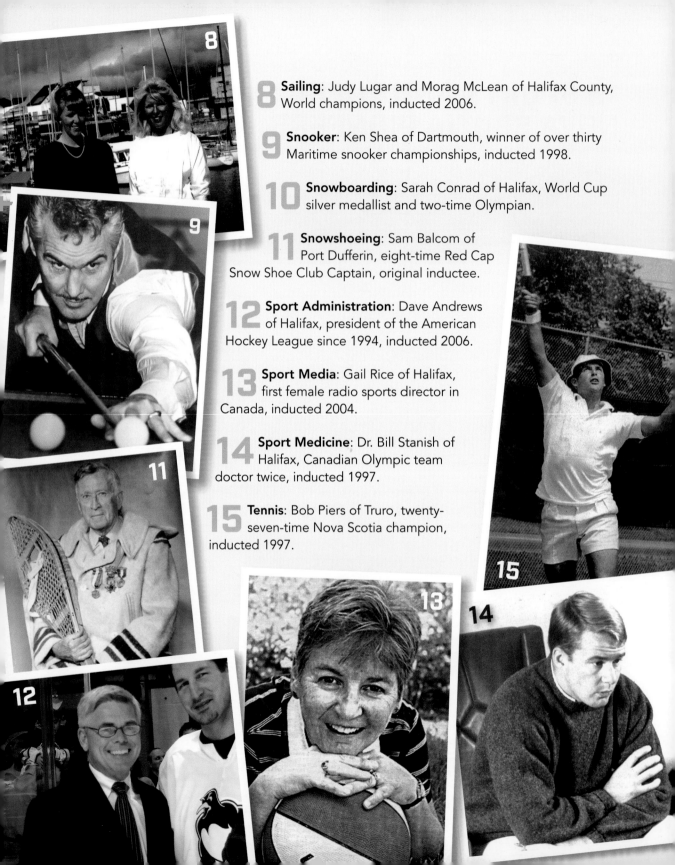

8 Sailing: Judy Lugar and Morag McLean of Halifax County, World champions, inducted 2006.

9 Snooker: Ken Shea of Dartmouth, winner of over thirty Maritime snooker championships, inducted 1998.

10 Snowboarding: Sarah Conrad of Halifax, World Cup silver medallist and two-time Olympian.

11 Snowshoeing: Sam Balcom of Port Dufferin, eight-time Red Cap Snow Shoe Club Captain, original inductee.

12 Sport Administration: Dave Andrews of Halifax, president of the American Hockey League since 1994, inducted 2006.

13 Sport Media: Gail Rice of Halifax, first female radio sports director in Canada, inducted 2004.

14 Sport Medicine: Dr. Bill Stanish of Halifax, Canadian Olympic team doctor twice, inducted 1997.

15 Tennis: Bob Piers of Truro, twenty-seven-time Nova Scotia champion, inducted 1997.

ELLIE BLACK

Halifax, Gymnastics
By Katie Tanner

Ellie Black has a magnetism that makes primary students and corporate CEOs alike listen wide-eyed when she speaks about her dedication to her sport. By the time she finishes her fiftieth photo of the day with young fans or signs her umpteenth autograph in an auditorium of students, her smile is just as warm and authentic as it was for the first person she met. Black comes across as a cheerful neighbour, a helpful teammate, or a welcoming friend while her name appears in headline after headline as she makes unprecedented leaps and bounds in women's gymnastics. When Black started gymnastics as a six year old, no one would have pegged her as a champion. At age nine, she finished last at her first competition and was second last at her second competition. But she tells her captive young audiences that those results were okay—because she knew she was improving.

Training out of Halifax's Alta Gymnastics under coaches Keiji Yamanaka and Hall of Famer David Kikuchi, Black competed at Elite Canada for the first time in 2009. She placed tenth in the all-around competition, but she asserted her talent for the vault by placing third in that event. The following year at the Canadian Championships, she finished fourteenth all-around, but repeated her third-place performance on the vault and achieved first place on the balance beam. At the 2010 Elite Canada competition, she moved up to second place on the vault.

In 2011, while preparing for the Canada Games, Black had her first major setback. An injury prevented her from competing in the games that were held in her hometown.

"I got injured right before the Canada Games in 2011," she recalls. "It was really heartbreaking because it was one of my first opportunities to show Canada what I can do. I took a lot away from that injury; I worked on my weaknesses, and it shaped me into the athlete I am today."

Returning to competition as a senior gymnast in 2012, Black captured first place in the vault event and was third in scoring on the beam at Elite Canada. She continued to gain momentum with her results in 2012, nabbing gold for her vault and floor routines at the Artistic Gymnastics World Cup and gold for vault and bronze for floor at the Canadian Championships, proving her strength in the vaulting event.

Black was then chosen for the 2012 Canadian Olympic gymnastics team, officially joining the squad only a couple weeks before the Games started in London. Her addition to the team made her the first Nova Scotian female gymnast to ever attend the Olympics. Black helped her team qualify for the team finals and she qualified for the individual vault finals.

Black contributed high scores in the vault, beam, and floor events, elevating the Canadian team to a fifth-place finish—the highest any Canadian gymnastics team has ever finished at the Olympics! Commentators remarked that the joy of the Canadian women's team at coming fifth was as exuberant as the first-place team's reaction to winning gold.

DID YOU KNOW?

- Black was the first non-American gold medallist in the women's Pan American all-around final since 1983.

- Black placed third all-around at the American Cup in 2016.

- Black is only the second Canadian ever to win a medal of any kind at the World Gymnastics Championships.

- Black has two siblings, and her younger brother, Will, is also a gymnast.

- In February 2018, Black was named co-winner, along with Brooklyn Moors, of the Canadian Senior Female Gymnast of the Year Award.

However, Black's celebration with the team was dampened by her struggles in the individual vault event. She injured her left ankle when landing her first vault, causing her to leave the second vault uncompleted.

Despite her disappointment, Black was not ready to give up competing. In 2013, she claimed bronze on beam and tied for silver on floor at the Summer Universiade, won the National all-around title, and competed in her first World Championships. From 2013 onward, her list of Elite Canada, Challenge Cup, and World Cup appearances and medals continues to grow and grow.

As Black continued to dominate women's gymnastics on an international level, she also completed her academic classes like any other teenager.

"I was still going to school and having a normal life and competing at that high level," she says. "I went to high school like everyone else."

Joining the Canadian team for the 2014 Commonwealth Games, she finished fourth with the team and in the individual all-around, while collecting gold on beam, silver on vault, and bronze on floor. Black then returned to the World Championships to record the highest-ever placement (ninth place) by a Canadian in a World or Olympic all-around final. She also repeated her Canadian Championships all-around win and brought home gold, silver, and bronze from the Pacific Rim Championships.

By 2015, now a kinesiology student at Dalhousie University, Black was on fire. She cinched her third consecutive National all-around title at the Canadian Championships, led the Canadian team to a sixth-place finish at the World Championships while climbing to a seventh-place all-around individual result, and became Canada's most decorated athlete at the Pan American Games in Toronto.

Black was a local hero when she returned from Toronto with five medals around her neck—three gold (for all-around, beam, and floor), one silver (for team), and one bronze (for vault).

Her climb to this point was the result of endless hard work, sacrificing so much of her life to train constantly. Black had painstakingly

TAKE THEIR WORD FOR IT

Ellie's best athletic attributes are her burning desire to be her best and her dedication to getting there. She is an inspiration to gymnasts across the country, but nowhere more than in Nova Scotia.

—David Kikuchi, Black's coach, Olympian and Hall of Famer

built every mile of her road to Rio and the 2016 Olympics. At the Games, Black fell off the beam during her routine, and, due to mistakes from other team members as well, Canada did not advance to the team finals. Black overcame her nerves, though, and gave a memorable individual performance in all four events, finishing a historic and unparalleled fifth in the individual all-around. After claiming that Olympic milestone for Canadian women, Black started 2017 with another injury that forced her to sit out the Elite Canada competition, but she bounced back quickly with her fourth Canadian all-around title in the spring. She capped off 2017 with her most impressive achievement yet—a silver all-around medal at the World Championships in Montreal, making her the first Canadian, male or female, to win an all-around medal at Worlds.

While Black, still just twenty-two, has charted previously unknown territory for Canadian gymnasts, topping podiums more than any other female from this country in her sport, her biggest impact may be the continued motivation her story brings to young Nova Scotians. Both girls and boys nervously wait to meet her as she spends some of her few hours outside the gym presenting to schools and community groups. Kids clutch drawings of their hero as they explain how Black's success has taught them to never give up.

"I am very excited to hopefully inspire younger kids and athletes to go for their dreams and not be afraid," says Black, whose fearless approach to competition lets Nova Scotians dream big with her every day.

15 GREAT NOVA SCOTIAN ATHLETES UNDER THE AGE OF 25

1 **Teni Akindoju**: soccer star who has represented Canada at both the Under-15 and Under-17 levels. Now playing in the Vancouver Whitecaps system.

2 **Karlee Burgess**: two-time Canadian Junior Curling champion and 2016 and 2018 World Junior Curling champion.

3 **Kristin Clarke**: two-time Canadian Junior Curling champion and 2016 and 2018 World Junior Curling champion.

4 **Nate Darling**: member of the Canadian team that won the 2017 FIBA Under-19 World Cup of Basketball. Now in his second year with the University of Alabama Birmingham.

5 **Kai Dwyer**: second-place finisher at the 2017 Canadian National Trampoline Championships.

6 **Jade Hannah**: winner of three gold medals and one bronze at the 2017 World Junior Swimming Championships.

7 **Georgia Lewin-LaFrance**: Canadian national sailing champion. She and partner Madeline Gillis finished sixth in their category at the 2017 Youth World Sailing Championship.

8 **Nathan MacKinnon**: high-scoring forward for the NHL's Colorado Avalanche and former Halifax Mooseheads star.

9 **Julie Moore**: star rookie with Dalhousie Tigers women's volleyball program.

10 **Mackenzie Myatt**: National silver medallist in mountain biking and a Canada Games silver medallist.

11 **Ryan O'Neil**: two-time tae kwon do World champion and National karate champion.

12 **Alex Scott**: member of Canada's national sprint kayak team.

13 **Craig Spence**: member of Canada's national sprint canoe team.

14 **Lindell Wigginton**: member of the Canadian team that won the 2017 FIBA Under-19 World Cup of Basketball. Now a rookie starting guard with Iowa State University.

15 **Blayre Turnbull**: member of 2018 Canadian Olympic women's hockey team that won silver. Played collegiate hockey at the University of Wisconsin.

KAREN FURNEAUX

Waverley, Sprint Kayaking, Inducted 2016
By Katie Tanner

Karen Furneaux has two World Championships titles in sprint kayak and three Olympic appearances under her belt. She has a successful wellness and leadership-training business built on her athletic experiences. She has an undaunted sense of positivity that rubs off on everyone she meets, and she has an indescribable quality that makes it all possible.

"She has the 'it,'" says Hall of Famer Frank Garner, who is chair of the International Canoe Federation Sprint Committee and who worked on sport psychology with Furneaux. "It's really that steely determination that says 'I want to reach the goal, I want to win and nothing's going to stop me' and that's what she's got. There was just no stopping her. You just knew she was on a fast track."

Always enthralled with sport and watching the Olympics on TV, Furneaux started out in figure skating, ski racing, gymnastics, and swimming.

"I just wanted to do it all," she says.

She started paddling in war canoe at age twelve as an extension of her participation in swimming at Cheema Aquatic Club.

"I loved being with my friends competing on the water outside," recalls Furneaux. "I liked the idea of making my boat go fast."

She remembers a particular race in Windsor at Pisiquid Canoe Club during her first days of bantam competition, where she had to race in a blue jug boat with no steering and ended up doing the whole race in a zigzag.

This is just one example of how she never let an obstacle hold her back.

Furneaux's long-time coach, Csom Latorovszki, explains how Furneaux would insist on redoing a practice piece until she completed it under her goal time. "She never gave up. She would fight until she was able to do it."

She paddled six days a week in the morning and evening, with weight training in the afternoon, all while taking full-time classes at Dalhousie.

"It's not easy to go out every day, sometimes twice a day, and push the limit," adds Latorovszki. "She pretty much never complained. I think her personality was a big part of her success. She really, really always brightened up the practice."

In 1993, Furneaux went to the Junior World Championships in the Czech Republic at age sixteen.

TAKE THEIR WORD FOR IT

"I think what marks her as different from other people, who just constantly work hard, is that she's usually smiling or she's doing it with grace and she's doing it with poise. She's just loving it....Nationally, racing against Karen, everybody knew that if you weren't off the line with her in the first 200 metres, you probably weren't going to be catching her any time soon."

—Jill D'Alessio, member of Furneaux's 2004 Olympic K4 crew

"That is where I really knew I wanted to represent Canada at the Olympics someday," she says.

After the 1993 Junior Worlds, Furneaux came home and raced at the Canadian Championships and won, knowing that her K1 had improved a lot.

As she improved, coming second in K1 at the 1994 World Cup, Furneaux started getting interested in comparing her times to other paddlers.

"My brain started to work [on] how to close that gap."

In 1998, Furneaux had the pleasure of beating the Hungarians in Hungary at the World Championships during the last race of the regatta, winning gold in the K2 200-metres. This achievement was followed by two golds at the 1999 Pan Am Games and her first Olympic competition in 2000, where she had a fifth-place finish in the K2 500-metre event.

In 2001, she finally single-handedly closed the gap on the world's fastest paddlers and won a World Championship in the K1 200-metre event following a season-long winning streak.

"It was a near perfect race," says Furneaux, who has reached perfection many times in her career of nine World Championship medals and fifty World Cup podium finishes.

"I was really lucky that I had a lot of sponsors and support," says Furneaux, who is also very grateful for the support she received from her parents, her training partners, and her coach and mentor Latorovszki.

Despite multiple injuries during her years of international competition, Furneaux qualified for the Olympics twice more and proved her dominance at the 2005 World Championships when she medalled in every distance in the singles (K1) discipline.

Latorovszki comments, "She was one of the smallest athletes on

DID YOU KNOW?

- Furneaux has been named Nova Scotia Female Athlete of the Year five times.

- Furneaux was ranked second in the world after 2005.

- Furneaux competed in gymnastics before she took up kayaking.

- Furneaux ran cross-country in her first year at Dalhousie University.

- When she is working with clients through I Promise Performance or talking to audiences at school presentations and speaking engagements, Furneaux uses an acronym to outline her approach to success—DREAM:
    D – determination
    R – role models
    E – expectations
    A – attitude
    M – momentum

the international field, but she sent out a message: it's not about the size; it's about the fight. She had one of the biggest hearts on the international field."

Now president of her company, I Promise Performance, Furneaux says, "My sport and my entrepreneurism are kind of the same—you're creating momentum and creating a plan."

She counts herself fortunate to be able to share her experiences with kids as a professional speaker and as an ambassador for the Hall of Fame's education program.

Her advice to the next generation of athletes is: "To set some clear goals but also have some good intentions. It's important to set goals, but not at the expense of what your intention is."

"Sport for me really was a door opener," she adds. "It let me be who I needed to be. It helped me to focus and develop my personality and confidence as a young girl. I use my learnings from sport experiences every single day."

15 NOVA SCOTIAN WOMEN WHO MADE THEIR MARK IN SPORT

1 **Sarah Baker**: multi-sport, three-time Paralympic medallist, inducted 2017.

2 **Julie Barton**: table tennis, youngest competitor in history to hold both the junior and senior Canadian singles titles, inducted 2012.

3 **Marie McNeil Bowness**: figure skating, winner of Canadian senior ice dance championships with Rob McCall in 1981, inducted 1996.

4 **Janice Cossar**: multi-sport, three-time CIS soccer All-Canadian, inducted 2010.

5 **Amy Cotton**: judo, two-time Olympian, inducted 2017.

6 **Ann Dodge**: paddling, Olympian, gold medallist in Canadian Championships war canoe and K4, inducted 1994.

7 **Chelsey Gotell**: swimming, three-time Paralympian with three gold, two silver, and seven bronze Paralympic medals.

8 Vida Large: badminton and tennis, once fifth-ranked player in singles badminton in Canada, inducted 1980.

9 Rita Lohnes: golf, once third-ranked junior golfer in Canada, inducted 1982.

10 Susan Mason MacLeod: swimming, first Nova Scotian swimmer to win a medal at the Canada Games, inducted 1985.

11 Karen Fraser Moore: volleyball, member of Canada's national women's volleyball program for six years, AUAA MVP in 1986, inducted 1996.

12 Marie Moore: swimming, Olympian, Pan American bronze medallist, inducted 1995.

13 Kathy Powers: golf, fourteen-time Nova Scotia Amateur Women's champion, inducted 2004.

14 Kathy MacCormack Spurr: basketball, AUS All Star and All-Canadian with the Dalhousie Tigers, a member of the Canadian national women's basketball team from 1985 to 1992, inducted 2001.

15 Jillian Saulnier: hockey, two-time silver medallist with team Canada at the IIHF World Championships and a member of the 2018 Canadian women's Olympic hockey team that won silver.

MARK SMITH

Halifax, Softball, Inducted 2002

By Joel Jacobson

The old story goes that a softball batter took a called ball. The catcher complained to the umpire who said, "It was low." The batter chimed in, "It sounded low to me, too, ump," knowing the pitch was almost impossible to see.

Mark Smith threw an awful lot of "sounded" pitches in his twenty-five-year career as one of the best softball pitchers in creation. The left-hander threw hard. He threw accurately. And he piled up a lot of wins for his teams.

Batters (we won't call them hitters because they didn't hit very often against Smith) would probably tell you the ball smacked the catcher's glove before it left Smith's hand. He was that good.

Growing up near the Halifax Common in the 1960s, he watched his father, Bobby, pitch in Halifax softball leagues. Smith started pitching in youth softball. In 1976, the youngest on the team at seventeen, he earned a spot on the Nova Scotia squad at the 1976 National Junior Championships. With a recognized talent, Smith left home two years later to pitch in Ontario. Then he conquered the world.

From Venezuela to the Philippines and New Zealand, and throughout the United States, he won awards and trophies, and led teams to victories with his arm and his bat. Smith led teams to two International Softball Federation World Championships and was selected to the All-World team a record five times.

DID YOU KNOW?

- Smith played in nine ISC World Championships between 1981 and 1994.
- Smith once threw a pitch that was clocked at 109 mph.
- Smith brought home Pan American gold in 1979, 1983, 1991, and 1999.
- Smith was named outstanding player of the 1981 ISC World Championships.

He won four gold medals with Canada at Pan American Games, and, in 1979, pitched the first no-hitter in Pan Am Games history.

Smith was tough. Downright menacing, some said. Built more along the lines of a football linebacker at 6 foot, 225 pounds, he was an intimidating presence.

Along with his blazing speed was a touch of wildness. Wildness that froze hitters in the box. Wildness from a ninety-plus-mile-per-hour, under-the-chin rise ball that made batters creep to the outer reaches of the box—for safety's sake.

When Smith, then twenty-two, arrived in California to pitch for the Camarillo Kings in 1981, "You couldn't dig in against him," said one opposition batter. "He was wild and very intimidating. He had that old pitcher's mentality, 'if you dig in against me, you're fair game.'" And the fairest of the game were the slap hitters. Running up in the box on Smith often got the slappers a closer-than-wanted look at his inside rise ball.

"Terry Canale was the first slapper I faced," says Smith. "He wasn't a very big guy. I used intimidation, throwing rise balls up and in to brush him off the plate. Once I got it into his head that if he committed early he might get hit, it threw off his timing and I was able to exploit that."

Jerry Hoffman, another opponent, agrees. "He threw so hard that you didn't dare dig in. I remember a rise ball inside he threw to Canale. Terry ducked and it went right over his head. The ball hit the backstop and bounced all the way to the outfield."

Smith spent two years in Camarillo, arguably the two best years of his softball-playing life. He called it "an experience in life skills."

"As a young Black kid from eastern Canada, I learned so much more about life than winning softball games," says Smith.

Smith returned to Canada in 1985 hoping to raise the profile of softball in Nova Scotia. In 1993, Smith and Keith's Breweries signed a three-year commitment in which he would play and coach for the Keith's team. In 1997, he and former junior teammate Gord Rudolph, by then a successful dentist and entrepreneur, established the Halifax Jaguars.

The following summer, Smith completed his playing career while also coaching the Jaguars to his first Senior Men's Canadian Championship gold medal.

Rudolph says his friend and former teammate was "exceptionally talented."

"As a junior, he became our best pitcher at seventeen, with a desire to win and a serious competitiveness. He was an obvious star in the making."

The oldest of five children, Smith had the advantage of two parents who offered tremendous support to all their kids.

"A good family structure translates into good things for people who are talented. All five Smith kids have done well as adults," says Rudolph.

He also praises Smith's ability to communicate. "As a player and now as a coach and administrator, he is a leader because of how well he deals with people."

Fellow inductee Todd King played on that Jaguars team in between travelling to play a stellar third base for Canadian national teams and American club teams.

"Perhaps Mark's greatest gift to the game is his mentoring ability," says King. "I have had some excellent coaches and mentors throughout my career. However, there is no question that Mark Smith is the single largest reason for my success."

Ann Dodge, a world-class Nova Scotian paddler and an inductee in the Hall of Fame, has been married to Smith for almost thirty years.

She says: "Mark has always worked to be the best: the best athlete and coach, of course, but the best husband, father [they have a twenty-three-year-old daughter, Jasmine, an Acadia graduate now studying at Mount Saint Vincent], employee—the best at whatever he does."

She says he does everything with a calm, positive attitude. "If there's something to overcome, he'll find a way. He doesn't allow things to get the better of him."

Working at various jobs during his playing and early coaching career, Smith was with the provincial Department of Justice, CEO of

TAKE THEIR WORD FOR IT

Mark Smith is quite possibly the best fast-pitch softball player of all time. His combination of overpowering pitching, clutch hitting and, most importantly, his ability to deliver when the game is on the line made him an overpowering opponent. Mark is a student of the game and always had a desire to learn more and push himself and those around him to be better.

—Todd King, Nova Scotia Sport Hall of Fame and Canadian Softball Hall of Fame inductee

MARK
SMITH

the Halifax Community YMCA, and then worked in various administrative capacities at Sport Nova Scotia.

Today, he's exclusively with Softball Canada as high-performance director and head coach of the women's national softball program. His 2015 team won gold at the Pan American Games and is now ranked third in the world while gearing up for participation at the 2020 Olympics.

Smith is a member of the Nova Scotia Sport Hall of Fame, Canadian Softball Hall of Fame, and American Softball Hall of Fame (ISC).

15 GREAT NOVA SCOTIAN CHAMPIONSHIP TEAMS

1 **1876 four-oared crew of Caleb Nickerson, Jack Nickerson, Obed Smith, and Warren Smith.** Won the World championship four-oared race despite a collision, but were stripped of their championship title after the English crew from London protested to the judges.

2 **Halifax Curling Club men's team of Jim Donahoe, Cliff Torey, Al MacInnes, Murray Macneill, and Harry Pyke.** Won the first Macdonald Brier Tankard for the Canadian Curling Championships in 1927.

3 **1935 Halifax Wolverines hockey team.** Became the first Nova Scotia team to win the Allan Cup, the title for the national senior hockey champions.

4 **1937 New Glasgow High School track and field team.** Won first place overall at the Canadian Junior Track and Field Championships, including seven first-place finishes and three second-place finishes for individual events.

5 **1957 Shearwater Flyers football team.** Won the Dominion of Canada Football Championship (the first Maritime team to do so) in front of a home crowd of 5,000 fans.

6 **1973 Saint Mary's men's football team.** Became the first Atlantic university team to win a national college football playoff championship involving representatives from all intercollegiate leagues.

7 **1973 Saint Mary's men's basketball team.** Won the CIS Championship, with Mickey Fox scoring 39 points in the final.

8 **1977 Cheema canoe team.** Became the first Atlantic Division canoe club to win the Canadian Championships.

9 **1977 Acadia men's basketball team**. Won the CIS Championship, hosted at the Halifax Forum, after winning 25 of the 30 games that season.

10 **Acadia women's varsity swim team**. Won CIS Championships in 1977 and 1978.

11 **Sailing team of Glen Dexter, Andreas Josenhans, and Sandy MacMillan**. Won World Sailing Championships in 1977 and 1980.

12 **1982 Dalhousie women's volleyball team**. Won the CIS Championship, becoming the only Atlantic university volleyball team to ever do so.

13 **1987 Glace Bay Colonels Little League baseball team**. Won the Canadian Championship and went on to place fifth in the Little League World Series.

14 **1995 Dalhousie men's soccer team**. Won the first, and to date only, CIS Championship for a Nova Scotia men's university soccer team.

15 **Colleen Jones curling rink of Jones, Nancy Delahunt, Mary-Anne Arsenault, and Kim Kelly**. Won five Canadian Championships (four consecutively) and two World Championships between 1999 and 2004.

STEVE GILES

**Lake Echo, Sprint Canoeing,
Inducted 2012**

By Bruce Rainnie

It was the very definition of an inauspicious start.

Had you seen his debut race, you might never have predicted that Steve Giles would go on to become one of this country's greatest-ever canoeists. He was ten years old at the time, and the setting was Lake Banook in Dartmouth….

"It was back when there was a seawall along the far side of the lake, before they built any sort of boardwalk," Giles remembers. "Just before the race began, this big gust of wind grabbed me and started pushing me and my canoe toward the wall. I could feel it happening but wasn't strong enough to stop it. A police boat had to rescue me! The only saving grace was that, as

C-1   MEN   1000 M

the boat pulled up, I saw my buddy Corey sitting there looking a tad embarrassed too. I knew the same thing had happened to him. So, in my very first race in a canoe, I never got off the line!"

Things would improve quickly for the young man from Lake Echo. Paddling out of the Orenda Canoe Club and under the guidance of coach Tony Hall, Giles first made noise nationally when, at the age of fourteen, he won C1 (single paddler), C2 (team of two), and C4 (team of four) events in the midget division of Nationals.

Then, in 1989, he made international noise, winning gold in the C1 1,000-metre race at the World Junior Championships. He followed that in 1993 with a bronze medal in the C1 500-metre at the senior World Championships in Copenhagen, Denmark. He had served notice that he had arrived, and would be a name worth watching. There was, however, a major obstacle standing between Giles and real international comfort and success. That obstacle? Nerves. Big-time, incapacitating nerves.

"It was so bad that I would literally throw up before big races, sometimes even on the start line," says Giles. "It reached the point that I started to really hate racing. I loved the training and the fitness and the feeling of being on the water, but I began to really detest the sickness I would feel on race day. It was after the 1997 World Championships in Dartmouth that I realized I would need some help to continue in the sport."

That help came in the form of one of the country's best-known sport psychologists, Penny Werthner. Through much discussion and hard work, she was able to convince Giles to focus on only what he could control, and not to worry about opponents or results.

"She made me account for every second of the race, so I knew what I should be focusing on at the 100-metre mark, the 150, the 200 and onward," recalls Giles. "I had my race plan and that was all I was concerned about. After about a year of that sort of detailed approach, I was actually able to relax more, enjoy my surroundings, and really race in the canoe. It was liberating."

With his mind now freer, incredible results began to follow. At the 1998 World Championships in Hungary, Giles was able to fend off his long-time rival, Martin Doktor of the Czech Republic, and win gold in the C1 1,000-metre event. As he raced toward the finish, words from his new bride, Angela, were racing through his mind.

"Doktor had come from behind to beat me at a race a few months earlier," says Giles. "Angela had spent a lot of money to travel and be there and she said to me, sort of jokingly, 'Why did you let that guy catch up to you and pass you like that? That isn't fun to watch.' So, in the last 250 metres of the Worlds, I saw Doktor a lane over and he was starting to gain on me. But I thought of what Angela might say, and I somehow found another gear. I didn't want to answer her tough questions again!"

With his win at the 1998 Worlds fresh in his mind, Giles went to the 2000 Olympics in Sydney, Australia, a favourite to reach the podium. And he did not disappoint, finishing third and winning a bronze medal. He describes that day as one of the finest of his career.

"There's always a bit of mixed emotion when you come away with a bronze medal," he says. "But on that day, it was the best I could do. I gave it my all and was really happy with the race. That's all you can really ask for. I would have been really disappointed had my career ended without an Olympic medal, so that race in Australia remains really special for me."

Giles would add another World Championships medal to his resume in 2002, this one a bronze. He would then compete in his fourth and final Olympic Games in Athens in 2004 (placing fifth in the final), before retiring after a storied sixteen-year career with the Canadian national team.

His career was defined by a dedication to training (five to six hours a day year-round) and an approach always rooted in humility. He was described by friends and teammates as "a modest, generous guy who didn't wear his elite athlete status." Giles says his approach came from lessons instilled by his parents, Mary and Peter.

"They always stressed schooling first of all. They

TAKE THEIR WORD FOR IT

When I received the call that morning in summer 1998 that Stevie had won the World championship in Szeged, the caller spoke of the incredible effort they had witnessed—the ability to keep the boat moving between the strokes with a different relationship with the water than many of the bigger, stronger competitors. They asked me if I was disappointed not to have been there to see it. I answered that I had seen it, played out day after day since Steve was eleven years old.

—Tony Hall, Giles's coach and Nova Scotia Sport Hall of Fame inductee

said I could paddle only if my marks were excellent. And because I loved to paddle, I became a really good student. They also demanded that I compete fairly and in the most sportsmanlike way possible. I tried to be as good a loser as I was a winner. And I always tried to live my athletic life like my regular, everyday life. No flies on Mom and Dad—I was very, very lucky to have them as my guides."

Giles and Angela are now guides to two children of their own. They enjoy paddling but are unlikely to follow in their father's footsteps.

"They like it, but aren't obsessed like I was," says Giles. "And that's okay. They have other passions and that's great."

But do they know how great their dad once was in a canoe?

"Of course," says Giles with a wink. "I tell them all the time!"

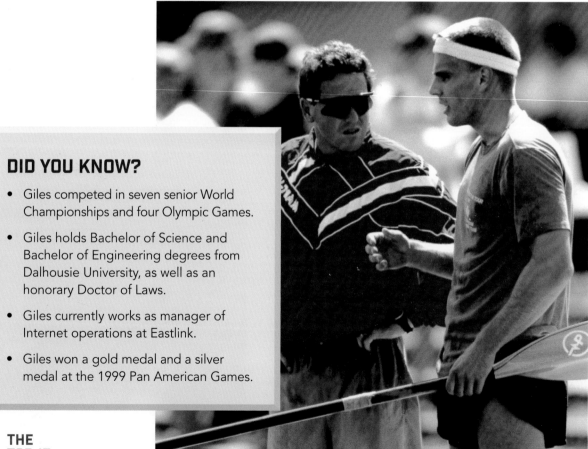

DID YOU KNOW?

- Giles competed in seven senior World Championships and four Olympic Games.

- Giles holds Bachelor of Science and Bachelor of Engineering degrees from Dalhousie University, as well as an honorary Doctor of Laws.

- Giles currently works as manager of Internet operations at Eastlink.

- Giles won a gold medal and a silver medal at the 1999 Pan American Games.

15 HISTORIC PLACES IN NOVA SCOTIA SPORT

1 **Acadia University in Wolfville**: home to the Acadia Relays, an annual interscholastic track event that began in 1926.

2 **Al MacInnis Sports Centre in Port Hood**: formerly known as the Port Hood Arena until Hall of Famer and NHL star Al MacInnis raised a quarter of a million dollars to save the complex from closure.

3 **Annapolis Royal**: where a section of the Governor's Gardens at the British Garrison Grounds was converted into Canada's first lawn bowling green in 1734.

4 **Antigonish**: home to the annual Highland Games since 1863.

5 **Cape Breton Highlands Golf Course in Ingonish Beach**: designed by world-renowned golf course architect Stanley Thompson and rated by *Sports Illustrated* as his most influential course.

6 **Halifax Forum**: the first artificial ice surface east of Montreal, opened 1927.

7 **Halifax Public Gardens**: the site of Canada's first skating rink in 1863 and the first public lawn tennis court in the country in 1876. A training spot for Hall of Fame rowers George Brown and John O'Neill and a meeting spot for cycling, snowshoeing, croquet, and archery clubs. Opened in the 1840s.

8 **Lake Banook in Dartmouth**: home to three canoe/kayak clubs, rowing clubs, and the site of Natal Day sport events since 1904.

9 **Lunenburg**: birthplace of the world-famous *Bluenose* racing schooner.

10 **Long Pond in Windsor**: believed to be the "Birthplace of Canadian Hockey," also known as "The Cradle of Hockey."

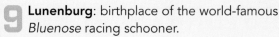

11 **Mayflower Curling Club**: founded in 1905; building used as a morgue for *Titanic* victims in 1912 before it was destroyed in the Halifax Explosion in 1917.

12 **McNabs Island and the Studley Quoit Club in Halifax**: important sites in the development of the popularity of quoits. Records of the sport on McNabs Island date to 1762; the Studley Club at the corner of what is now Dalhousie's Studley Campus was founded in 1858.

13 **New Waterford**: home to the New Waterford Coal Bowl Classic, a national invitational boys' high school basketball tournament that began in 1982.

14 **Truro Raceway**: home to harness racing since 1875 and also the site of the annual Nova Scotia Provincial Exhibition.

15 **Wanderers Grounds**: used since the 1880s by the Halifax Wanderers Amateur Athletic Club for rugby, lawn bowling, and more; also the former home of the Navy clubhouse and many Halifax & District League baseball games.

AILEEN MEAGHER

Halifax, Track & Field, Original Inductee

By Katie Tanner

Aileen Meagher likely didn't grow up with dreams of running at the Olympics. In the 1920s, women were still fighting for their rights at a time when many doctors believed that the competition would put too much strain on a woman's "inner workings." In 1928, the Olympic Committee decided that women could compete in track and field events for the first time, yet Nova Scotian track star Gertrude Phinney was still denied her well-earned spot on the team due to fears about her feminine constitution.

Needless to say Meagher didn't have many predecessors after whom to model her athletic career, so she just had to be the first. The first Nova Scotian woman to compete for Canada at the Olympic Games. The first Nova Scotian woman to win an Olympic medal. The record setter for women's track on a provincial and national level. Meagher was a pioneer for Canadian women in athletics.

The trailblazer had a slow start though, having never run a track meet until she was enrolled at Dalhousie University. However, Meagher's late introduction to running was the only slow thing about her story, as her natural talent was undeniable from the time she set foot on a track.

By 1930, at age twenty, Meagher held the Canadian records in the 100- and 220-yard events. It would take over three decades for another Nova Scotia-born Olympian, Debbie Miller Brown, to match and break Meagher's 100-yard dash time of 11.2 seconds.

Local lore has it that physical educator Edgar Stirling, watching Meagher race at the intramural meet he had organized on the Dalhousie track in 1931, saw her potential and suggested she train for the Olympics that were to take place in Los Angeles only eighteen months later.

Meagher won the 220-yard dash at the 1932 Olympic trials in Hamilton, Ontario. Unfortunately, the Olympic Committee decided not to include the women's 220-yard event in the Olympic program. Team Canada's decision to then remove Meagher from the Olympic contingent reportedly resulted in much controversy stemming from Maritime sports officials' objections. She was subsequently named to the national relay team and began training for the Olympics with Coach Stirling.

While injury prevented Meagher from running at the 1932 Games, she had cemented her place as a national powerhouse in track and field.

An Amateur Athletic Union of Canada certificate issued in 1934 states that Meagher also set a national 200-metre dash record in

DID YOU KNOW?

- Meagher showcased her artwork at a variety of exhibitions beginning in 1952.

- Meagher matched the Canadian record in the 100-yard dash when she won the event title at the 1937 Maritime Championships.

- While the 100-yard dash is no longer an event in Canadian women's athletics, the current 100-metre record holder only beats Meagher's record by 0.22 seconds.

- Aileen Meagher Track Classic director and fellow Hall of Famer Kevin Heisler says he named the meet after Meagher in the style of Vancouver's Harry Jerome International Track Classic, in the hopes that the name of a Nova Scotia sport celebrity would attract more runners.

- Meagher received the Dalhousie Award in 1972 and was inducted into Canada's Sports Hall of Fame in 2015.

1933 of 25.4 seconds. In 1934, she went to the British Empire Games in London and won three medals: silver in the 220-yard sprint and 3x110/220-yard relay, and gold in the 4x110/220-yard relay.

Meagher continued to dominate in 1935, winning provincial and Maritime honours and capping off her running season with double national titles, winning the 100-metre and 200-metre events at the Women's Dominion Track and Field Championships in Montreal.

Meagher's outstanding performances in 1935 were recognized with three prestigious awards: the Velma Springstead Trophy for Most Outstanding Female Athlete in Canada, the Bobbie Rosenfeld Award for Canada's Female Athlete of the Year as named by The Canadian Press, and the Norton Crow Memorial Award for Amateur Athlete of the Year.

Most notably, the Crow Award was originally created by the Amateur Athletic Union of Canada, and the Women's Amateur Athletic Federation believed there was a slim chance of it going to a female recipient (Crow himself had never been a strong supporter of women's sport). Rumour has it that newspapers reported Meagher's win as the first and last time a woman would nab the prize. While proof of these headlines isn't available, two things are apparent: Meagher had made it clear that women were a force to be reckoned with in sport and she

AILEEN
MEAGHER

continued to be the first in her field for many accomplishments. (The Crow Award was later reassigned to Outstanding Male Athlete of the Year at the Canadian Sports Awards.)

By 1935, Meagher had already begun her career as a schoolteacher at St. Patrick's in Halifax, but she was not ready to retire her running cleats. She made it onto the 1936 Canadian Olympic team with an exceptional performance at the Olympic trials and captured bronze with the 4x100 relay team at the Games in Berlin.

Meagher returned to the British Empire Games in 1938 to win bronze in the 4x110/220-yard relay and silver in the 3x110/220-yard event. Having always valued the travel that came with competitive running, Meagher left the Games in Australia with an around-the-world ticket and travelled for six months before returning to Halifax.

Retiring from running in 1938, Meagher became a full-time teacher and is fondly remembered for her commitment to young students. Her occupation also earned her the moniker of "The Flying Schoolmarm." Local accounts recall the Flying Schoolmarm running to school on a daily basis so she could save her tram fare to buy doughnuts.

All accounts of Meagher seem to capture her zest for life and a practicality that was never overshadowed by her celebrated victories. (She supposedly used her Olympic medal as a paperweight on her teacher's desk and was unworried when it went missing). She easily transitioned her natural talents to art and became a well-respected painter later in her life, encouraging her students to send their own artwork in to competitions.

Her legacy in Halifax, her home city for her entire life, lives on through the annual Aileen Meagher Track Classic, which hosts budding male and female track stars from around the world in Halifax each year. Now, ninety years since Meagher laced up her track shoes for the first time, these young sprinters will have someone to look up to, someone who paved the way for Canadian women in track and field, someone who did it first.

TAKE THEIR WORD FOR IT

Sportswriters the world over know her as "Canada's Flying Schoolmarm," a laughing-eyed Irish colleen whose spiked shoes have sped over the cinder paths of Europe and North America. That's Aileen Meagher of Halifax, queen of Canadian girl sprinters.

—Alex Nickerson, Hall of Famer, sports journalist and founding member of the Nova Scotia Sport Hall of Fame, in the *Halifax Mail* July 24, 1937

AILEEN
MEAGHER

15 HALL OF FAMER NICKNAMES

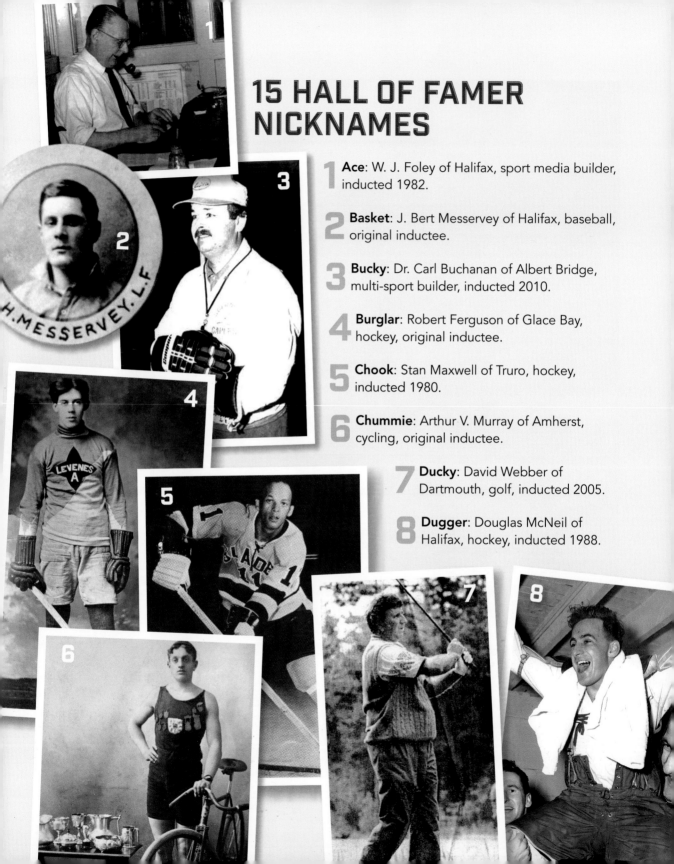

1 **Ace**: W. J. Foley of Halifax, sport media builder, inducted 1982.

2 **Basket**: J. Bert Messervey of Halifax, baseball, original inductee.

3 **Bucky**: Dr. Carl Buchanan of Albert Bridge, multi-sport builder, inducted 2010.

4 **Burglar**: Robert Ferguson of Glace Bay, hockey, original inductee.

5 **Chook**: Stan Maxwell of Truro, hockey, inducted 1980.

6 **Chummie**: Arthur V. Murray of Amherst, cycling, original inductee.

7 **Ducky**: David Webber of Dartmouth, golf, inducted 2005.

8 **Dugger**: Douglas McNeil of Halifax, hockey, inducted 1988.

9 **Ginny**: Virginia Smith of Yarmouth, swimming builder, inducted 2001.

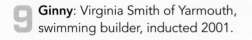

10 **Hum**: Ismet Joseph of Truro, baseball, inducted 1992.

11 **Red**: Bill Stuart of Amherst, hockey, original inductee.

12 **Rock-a-Bye**: George Ross of Marble Mountain, Inverness County, boxing, inducted 1983.

13 **Sugar Ray**: Raymond Downey of Halifax, boxing, inducted 2015.

14 **The Oxford Street Trophy Room**: the home of Gladys and Annie Longard of Halifax, badminton builders, inducted 1988.

15 **The Seven Survivors**: the 1931 Truro Bearcats hockey team (the players who remained for playoffs following the disqualification of several players), inducted 1980.

JOHNNY MILES

Sydney Mines, Track and Field, Original Inductee
By Katie Tanner

Johnny Miles holds more than a spot in Nova Scotia's sport history—he has a special place in Nova Scotians' hearts. He is a shining example of humility, hard work, and raw talent, and he has one of the most inspiring underdog stories that the province has ever produced. Arguably the greatest distance runner to ever represent Nova Scotia,

Miles conquered the world's most famous marathon not once, but twice, beating the odds and cementing his legacy.

Born in Halifax, England, in 1905, Miles was a small child when his family moved to Nova Scotia. Many Cape Breton communities are eager to claim a piece of the Miles narrative. He is listed in the Florence census around the time that he started running (sixteen years old), and North Sydney and Sydney Mines are listed as his hometown in records of his international competitions. Whichever hamlet he called home in the 1920s, Miles was about to make Cape Breton and Nova Scotia part of the regular vocabulary of sports commentators throughout North America.

In his earliest races, Miles placed third in the 1922 North Sydney three-mile race and fourth in the Sydney Mines three-mile race of the same year. By 1925, he had climbed from sixteenth place to first in the Sydney Victoria Day Race, had won the six-mile Dartmouth Natal Day Race and the ten-mile Halifax Modified Marathon, and he had claimed the title of Canadian champion in the five-mile event.

Miles's marked improvement over only three years was a result of his unusual training methods, many of which were created by his father, John Sr., who took a great interest in Miles's running career. Johnny worked as a grocery delivery boy and he would run alongside his horse as it pulled the wagon on his route, just part of the one hundred miles he ran per week. Sometimes Miles's father would drive the horse and wagon, forcing Miles to run faster to keep up. (Local legend states that John Sr. was often booed by residents who thought he was a cruel boss forcing his young employee to run beside the delivery wagon.)

After Miles took the 1925 Halifax Modified Marathon title, his father raised the money ($300 from their fellow Cape Bretoners) to pay the way to Boston to compete in the thirtieth annual Boston Marathon. Despite never having run a race longer than ten miles, Miles showed up in Boston with his father in 1926, confident that the twenty-six-mile victory was attainable.

TAKE THEIR WORD FOR IT

The remarkable life story and running accomplishments of Johnny Miles have inspired many Nova Scotians to live healthy active lifestyles and to volunteer in their communities and make them better places to live. Nowhere is this more evident than in Pictou County where the annual Johnny Miles Running Weekend is celebrated. Johnny Miles's life and legacy continues to have a positive impact on the quality of life in our communities and the health of our citizens.

—John Lynn, co-chairperson of the Johnny Miles Foundation

The marathon director scoffed at Miles's entry in the race when he heard that the Nova Scotian had never even seen a full marathon. Undeterred, Miles and his father walked the course the night before the race, but were concerned when they lost their way. A police officer informed them they needn't worry as Miles could just follow the crowd, but John Sr. insisted they understand the route, as he was certain that his son would be leading the pack of runners.

DID YOU KNOW?

- Miles is one of three Nova Scotians to win the Boston Marathon (Ronald J. MacDonald won in 1898 and Freddie Cameron won in 1910), but is the only Nova Scotian to win twice.

- The Johnny Miles Marathon was founded by Dr. Johnny Miles Williston, whose mother named him after Johnny Miles when Miles defeated DeMar and Michaelson in Glace Bay the day after Williston was born.

- When Miles won the 1929 marathon, he sent a telegram to his then-girlfriend and future wife, Bess, to inform her of his victory. He joked to reporters that maybe this win would be what he needed to get her to marry him.

- In the 1920s and '30s, Nova Scotia schools provided students with hygiene textbooks that featured Miles on the front cover, as he epitomized a fit and healthy lifestyle.

- The *Boston Globe* reported the following at the 1926 Boston Marathon:

"With no form to speak of, no particular training, and no experience whatsoever, this apple cheeked laddie from a province by the sea, paddling along in a pair of simple tennis shoes, wiping his nose now and then with a handkerchief his mother had pressed into his hand…smashed almost four minutes off the World Record set by DeMar in 1924 and almost 17 minutes off the Olympic record made by Stenroos in Paris."

Among the ninety-six racers at the starting line of the 1926 Boston Marathon were Clarence "DeMarathon" DeMar of Ohio, who had won four previous Boston Marathons, and Albin Stenroos of Finland, the 1924 Olympic marathon gold medallist. All bets were on one of these two well-known runners, and the naïve newcomer from Sydney Mines, with his handmade maple leaf shirt and ninety-eight-cent sneakers, was not even on the reporters' radar.

Half a million spectators watched in awe as Miles kept pace with the top runners. His father had advised him to stay with the leaders, so he did just that, following Stenroos when he pulled ahead of DeMar at the seven-mile mark. After overcoming a severe pain in his side, Miles passed Stenroos on the Newton Hills at the twenty-two-mile mark. Afraid that making eye contact with Stenroos would encourage the Finnish runner to engage in a duel, Miles never looked back, sprinting across the finish line with an incredible new course record of 2:25:40.4. By the time Stenroos crossed the line four minutes later, followed by DeMar, Miles was already in the showers and the reporters were scrambling to find out who he was.

Miles was welcomed home to Cape Breton by five thousand fans (twice the population of Sydney Mines), a live band, and the honorary title of "Public Friend #1." School was cancelled due to the celebrations. Meanwhile, Boston papers were still reporting on the "Unknown Kid" from Nova Scotia and speculating as to whether he was a one-time wonder or a potential repeat winner.

In 1927, Miles was ready to claim his second Boston Marathon victory, but his father unwittingly sabotaged his chances when he thought that shaving down the tread on Miles's cheap sneakers would make them more like an expensive lightweight pair. The scorching temperatures that day melted the road tar, which soon penetrated Miles's thin soles and burned his feet. Bleeding and devastated, Miles dropped out of the race by the seventh mile, receiving much ridicule from the papers.

One month after leaving the marathon unfinished, Miles had the chance to race DeMar and future Boston Marathon winner Whitey Michaelson at a fifteen-mile event in Glace Bay, winning the race and starting his journey of redemption.

The Canadian Olympic coach insisted that Miles take a year off from the Boston race to focus on the 1928 Olympics, at which Miles placed sixteenth, but Miles returned to the starting line of the world's premier marathon in 1929. Now living in Hamilton, Ontario, Miles travelled to Boston hoping to prove that he was not a quitter.

Miles started his third Boston Marathon in seventh place, trailing behind DeMar and a group of other notable international racers. At

JOHNNY MILES

twenty miles, painful heel and calf cramps plagued Miles, but he ran on his toes until the cramping passed. In the final miles he passed the two Finnish runners, who were favoured to win, and crossed the finish line first, two minutes and eighteen seconds ahead of the second-place racer. Miles's time was 2:33:08. He was honoured that year with the Will Cloney International Award for Sports.

Miles won a bronze medal at the 1930 British Empire Games and again represented Canada at the 1932 Olympics, placing fourteenth. He later received the Dalhousie Award, the Order of Canada, and induction into Canada's Sports Hall of Fame. Miles's legacy is most notably preserved by the annual Johnny Miles Marathon, which has brought as many as two thousand runners to New Glasgow, Nova Scotia, every year since 1975.

Miles was one of five Nova Scotians who finished in the top forty of the Boston Marathon in 1929, with fellow Cape Bretoner Billy Taylor in the top ten, but Miles had proved he was still the best, and the Nova Scotia racers who joined him that day were just the beginning of the many track athletes who would be inspired by Miles's accomplishments for decades to come.

15 NOVA SCOTIAN TRACK & FIELD STARS

1 **Cecilia Branch of Halifax**: national and international champion in the 100-metre hurdles, inducted 2001.

2 **Walter Dann of Halifax**: two-time Paralympic silver medallist, one for the 60-metre wheelchair sprint at the 1968 Games and one for the 4x60-metre wheelchair relay in 1972.

3 **Vern Eville, born in Manitoba and attended Acadia University**: represented Canada at the first Commonwealth Games and won five events at the 1928 Maritime Junior Championships, original inductee.

4 **Fred Fox of Lunenburg**: held a 100-yard record for twenty-eight years and won gold and bronze at the 1940 Coronation Games, inducted 1980.

5 **Geoff Harris of Halifax**: 2012 Canadian champion in the 800-metre event and Olympian at the 2012 Games in London.

6 **Jimmy Hawboldt of Westville**: known for defeating Johnny Miles in three of six races and for winning the *Evening News* five-mile race four times, inducted 1980.

7 **Jenna Martin of Liverpool**: 2011 and 2012 Canadian champion in the women's 400-metre event and Olympian at the 2012 Games in London.

8 **Robyn Meagher of Mulgrave**: two-time Olympian and a Commonwealth Games silver medallist, inducted 2010.

9 **Leigh Miller of Elmsdale**: once recognized as the fastest human being in the world, gold medal-winner at the British Empire Games in 1930, original inductee.

10 **Richard G. Munro of Bridgewater**: Canadian senior cross-country champion and four-time AUS cross-country champion, inducted 2014.

11 **Frank Nicks of Halifax**: silver medallist at the British Empire Games and named Nova Scotia's Outstanding Athlete of the Year in 1934, original inductee.

12 **Roy Oliver of New Waterford**: four-time winner of the *Herald and Mail* 10-mile marathon and provincial record-holder for the 10,000-metre event for forty years, inducted 1980.

13 **Gertrude Phinney of Lawrencetown, Annapolis County**: by winning the 220-yard event at the Canadian Championships, she qualified for the Olympic team, but wasn't allowed to compete due to physicians' misconceptions about female athletes in the 1920s, original inductee.

14 **Adrienne Power of Jeddore**: Olympian at the 2008 Beijing Games, two-time Commonwealth Games bronze medallist and two-time Canadian champion in the women's 200-metre.

15 **Earl Arthur Ryan of Antigonish**: Maritime champion in broad jump, triple jump, and pole vault, and Canadian champion in triple jump, inducted 1988.

GEORGE DIXON

**Africville, Halifax,
Boxing, Original Inductee**

By Steven Laffoley, with introduction by Bruce Rainnie

George Dixon was born in Africville on July 29, 1870. He was a boxing prodigy—anyone who saw him as a teenager realized he had a special gift. He was small and tough as nails. He stood only five foot three and weighed only eighty-seven pounds when he began his professional boxing career. He weighed no more than one hundred and eighteen pounds during his prime years.

His story is beautifully told in a book entitled *Shadowboxing: The Rise and Fall of George Dixon*. It was written by award-winning author Steven Laffoley, who has allowed us to use the following excerpt. Enjoy…

I was born at Halifax, Nova Scotia, in 1870, and when I was about eight years of age, my parents

moved to Boston. I received a public school education, having attended a Halifax school for two years. When about fourteen years of age I secured employment with a Boston photographer, and while there engaged, I first began to learn how to spar. I witnessed an exhibition one night at the Boston Music Hall, which was given by two local athletes, and the next day I purchased a book on boxing from which I gained much valuable information.
— George Dixon, A Lesson in Boxing *(1893)*

George Dixon was the finest boxer of his generation and arguably among the finest boxers ever. His accomplishments in the ring were extraordinary: the first Black boxing champion, the first Canadian champion, the first champion of multiple weight classes, and the first champion to lose and regain a title. In a twenty-year career, Dixon

DID YOU KNOW?

- Dixon fought in what is widely regarded as the longest boxing match ever. It occurred in February of 1890 against Cal McCarthy, bantamweight and featherweight champion of the eastern United States. They fought for seventy rounds in a bout that took *four hours.* After all of that, it was declared a draw!

- It is estimated Dixon earned close to $250,000 in his boxing career, which in 2018 dollars would be close to $7 million. But like many who acquire sudden wealth, he was unable to keep it. He liked fancy clothes, he liked to drink and gamble, and he was incredibly generous to charities. He died practically penniless at age thirty-seven.

- Dixon became the first-ever Black world boxing champion and the first Black athlete to hold a championship title in any American sport when he defeated Nunc Wallace for the bantamweight title in 1890. His first world title win, in 1888, was not recognized as a World Championship.

- Dixon won his second World Championship title in 1891 when he defeated Cal McCarthy, lost it in 1894, and reclaimed it against Dave Sullivan in 1898.

- Dixon had a vaudeville troupe called the "George Dixon Speciality Co.," which toured North America in the early 1890s.

- Dixon used his success to act as an advocate for the Black community, and, when New Orleans organizers asked Dixon to fight champion Jack Skelly in 1892, Dixon would only agree to the match if seven hundred seats were reserved for Black community members.

defended his title more than any other champion—then or since—and reportedly fought an unprecedented eight hundred bouts.

Making these accomplishments even more astonishing was the context within which these achievements were earned. In an age when Black men were routinely lynched for simply being Black, George Dixon publicly fought and beat hundreds of white boxers across America, Canada, and Europe. He even married a white woman.

So, too, George Dixon was a great innovator. As much as anyone, George Dixon defined what we recognize today as the sport of boxing, introducing and refining many training and fighting techniques still used more than one hundred years later. Long- and short-distance running, the punching bag, shadowboxing, and any number of combination punches and defensive manoeuvres—the list of Dixon's contributions to boxing is uniquely long.

Before Muhammad Ali and Joe Louis, before Sugar Ray Robinson and Jack Johnson, before Marvelous Marvin Hagler and Sugar Ray Leonard, before all the great Black boxing champions of every age and of every weight class, there was George Dixon.

He was the first. And he was the greatest.

Renowned boxing historian and *Ring Magazine* founder Nat Fleischer once said of Dixon, "For his ounces and inches, there was

never a lad his equal. Even in the light of the achievements of John L. Sullivan, the critics of his day referred to 'Little Chocolate' (Dixon) as the greatest fighter of all time. I doubt there was ever a pugilist who was as popular during his entire career. Dixon was a marvel of cleverness, yet he could hit and slug with the best of them."

Simply put, said Fleischer, "He had everything."

Sam Austin, the larger-than-life sports editor at America's first tabloid newspaper, the *Police Gazette*—which, more than any other newspaper of the era, helped take boxing from illegal backroom brawling to the most popular sport of the age—described George Dixon as "The Fighter Without a Flaw." In a long article, published in 1899, Austin wrote, "Even in the light of John L. Sullivan's splendid achievements in the ring, the fact cannot be disputed that the greatest fistic fighter, big or little, that the world has ever known is George Dixon."

But for all the accomplishments and adulation that George Dixon achieved and received in his lifetime, he died a beggar, in the alcoholic ward of New York's Bellevue Hospital—homeless, forgotten, and alone. It is just one of the many ironies of the complex man who was George Dixon.

Ironic, too, is that while George Dixon was being forgotten, George Dixon's archetypical story was taking hold of the public imagination—the familiar tale of a young Black man who, suffocating under the weight of poverty and racism, and withering in the heat of limited opportunities, uses his fists and wits to fight his way, against daunting, unrelenting challenges, to an extraordinary reward: Champion of the World. Along the way, he grows rich and famous and is loved by all. But then, as the now familiar story goes, he overreaches. He gambles, he drinks, and he lives the self-indulgent life of the "sport." Finally, as this story requires, he stays in the ring for one fight too many.

And he loses it all.

This story—the rise and fall of the Black boxer—has become cliché. Yet the rise and fall of George Dixon's life is, at the same moment, singularly different because his story was the first of its kind in modern

TAKE THEIR WORD FOR IT

"He was fast, tricky, combative, canny, courageous, a master in every respect of the art of self-defense, a great ring general. His left hand was one of the best in the business. His double to the body has never been equalled. His right was equally good."

—Nat Fleischer, founder of *Ring Magazine*

boxing. He followed no one. He cut his own path and created his own life. For this reason, his story—his triumphs and tragedies as well as his rise and fall—transcends the cliché.

Further, the real importance of George Dixon's life story lies not in the act of boxing itself, but in how, through the act of boxing, Dixon's unique life was distilled to the essence of human triumph and tragedy. Author and boxing aficionado Joyce Carol Oates once wrote, "Boxing is about being hit more than it is about hitting, just as it is about feeling pain, if not devastating psychological paralysis, more than it is about winning."

Life is like that. It is not so much about winning the fight as it is about taking the punch and carrying on. George Dixon's life is compelling because few boxers in the long history of the sport took a punch—literally and figuratively—as hard as he did and carried on so well.

GALLERY OF Champions

GEORGE DIXON

WORLD'S FEATHERWEIGHT CHAMPION

GEORGE DIXON

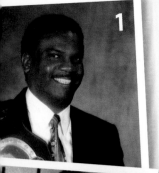

15 OTHER GREAT NOVA SCOTIA BOXING FIGURES

1 **Ricky Anderson of Africville in Halifax**: amateur record of 85 wins, 12 losses; professional record of 18 wins, 2 losses; former Canadian welterweight champion; two-time Nova Scotia Male Athlete of the Year, inducted 2003.

2 **Chris Clarke of Halifax**: 1975 Pan Am Games lightweight gold medallist (first Canadian boxer to win gold at the Pan Am Games); competed in the 1976 Summer Olympics; former Canadian welterweight champion; former Canadian middleweight champion, inducted 2006.

3 **Delmore William "Buddy" Daye of New Glasgow**: winner of the Canadian super featherweight title in 1964, the first African Nova Scotian sergeant-at-arms for the Nova Scotia House of Assembly, inducted 1981.

4 **Dave Downey of Halifax**: former two-time Canadian middleweight champion; professional record of 24 wins, 4 losses, 2 draws; fought professionally from 1960 to 1978, inducted 1999.

5 **Raymond "Sugar Ray" Downey of Halifax**: son of Dave Downey. Amateur record of 160 wins, 20 losses; bronze medallist at the 1988 Seoul Olympics; posted a 16-2-and-1 record as a professional, inducted 2015.

6 **Hubert Earle of Halifax**: world-class boxing official; first Canadian referee to be appointed by the New York State Athletic Commission to referee a main bout in Madison Square Garden; has refereed dozens of World Championship boxing matches; referee-in-chief of the Nova Scotia Combat Sports Authority, inducted 2011.

7 **Tyrone Gardiner of Sydney**: former Canadian lightweight champion (won title in 1963); professional record of 29-13-3; also held Maritime and Eastern Canadian titles, inducted 1980.

8 **Clyde Gray of Three Mile Plains**: former Canadian welterweight champion; former Commonwealth welterweight champion; fought three times for the World welterweight championship; compiled a professional record of 69 wins, 10 losses, and 1 draw, inducted 1983.

9 **Taylor Gordon of Halifax**: head coach or assistant coach for the Canadian national boxing team at seven Olympic Games; founder of the Citadel Amateur Boxing Club; has coached nine Nova Scotia boxers to Olympic Games; as an amateur fighter, posted a record of 101 wins and 10 losses, inducted 1996.

10 **Lawrence Hafey of New Glasgow**: brother of Art Hafey, won the Canadian middleweight title in 1975; fought 73 times, posting a record of 48-23-and-2; once went the distance at Madison Square Garden with three-time World Champion Wilfred Benitez; once boxed four times in twenty-seven days, inducted 2013.

11 **Richard "Kid" Howard of Terence Bay**: standing just five foot two, won the Maritime lightweight title in 1949 and the Canadian lightweight title in 1954; once ranked by *Ring Magazine* as the no. 6 lightweight in the world; fought professionally 108 times, with 77 wins, 26 losses, and 5 draws; was never knocked out, inducted 1982.

12 **Carroll Morgan of Antigonish**: represented Canada in the heavyweight division at the 1972 Munich Olympics, where he made it to the quarterfinals; three-time Canadian champion, four-time Atlantic champion, and seven-time provincial champion; never lost a fight to a fellow Canadian, inducted 2008.

13 **Blair Richardson of South Bar, Cape Breton**: former Canadian middleweight champion, former Commonwealth middleweight champion; professional record of 45 wins, 5 losses, and 2 draws, inducted 1980.

14 **George "Rock-A-Bye" Ross of Marble Mountain, Inverness County**: former Canadian middleweight champion; professional record of 43 wins, 6 losses, and 1 draw; once fought 14 times in a single year (1948), inducted 1983.

15 **Murray Sleep of Halifax**: former president of the Canadian Professional Boxing Federation; supervisor of championship fights for the World Boxing Association; former vice-president of the World Boxing Association, inducted 2005.

SAM LANGFORD

Weymouth Falls, Boxing, Original Inductee

By Bruce Rainnie

So the story goes something like this. The extraordinary young boxer Sam Langford was once again in the ring with a game but overwhelmed adversary. The promoter had begged Langford to keep the fight going for a while and not throw any knockout punches until after the seventh round. So as he walked out for the eighth round, after twenty-one minutes of gentle sparring, Langford reached out to touch gloves with the other boxer.

"What are you doing, Sam? It ain't the last round!" said the perplexed pugilist.

"'Tis for you son, 'tis for you," replied Langford, who promptly had his opponent looking up at the ceiling and seeing only stars.

Such was the genius of one of the greatest fighters in the history of the sport, and certainly the greatest never to have won a World boxing championship (more on that shortly).

Langford was born in Weymouth Falls, Nova Scotia, in March of either 1883, 1884, or 1885 (records are hazy and conflicting). His boxing story began when he left home at an early age to escape an abusive father. At around age fourteen, he was living in Boston and looking for work when he walked into a small drugstore. He asked the owner, Joe Woodman, for a job and told him he hadn't eaten for two days. Woodman gave him a meal and also offered him work as janitor at a boxing gym he operated on the side.

Langford quickly became obsessed with the sport. He watched the pro boxers, studied their styles, and began to spar with some of the best in the gym. He was a lightning-fast learner, and within a year had won the Amateur Featherweight Championship of Boston.

Langford was built to be a boxer. He stood only five foot seven but had a seventeen-inch neck, fifteen-inch biceps, a forty-three-inch chest and, most incredibly, a seventy-three-inch reach! He was short, stocky, long armed, and incredibly powerful. He was also smart and crafty, described by many as a boxing prodigy.

"He was quite possibly the greatest fighter who ever lived," says boxing historian Mike

TAKE THEIR WORD FOR IT

The hell I feared no man. There was one man I wouldn't fight because I knew he would flatten me. I was afraid of Sam Langford.

—Jack Dempsey, former World heavyweight champion

Silver. "He mastered every punch. His short hook on the inside and his right cross and uppercut were particularly deadly. His punishing jab was also one of the best. He was a strategist who knew how to manoeuvre, with the ability to explode out of an offensive or defensive position. Langford's every move embodied the technique of a studied master boxer. During his prime, he was rarely out-fought, out-thought, or out-punched."

Clay Moyle, author of *Sam Langford: History's Greatest Uncrowned Champion*, writes that "during the first quarter of the 20th century, the prospect of facing the five-foot-seven-inch dynamo, who weighed no more than 185 pounds at his peak, struck terror in the hearts of most of his contemporaries, including heavyweight champions Jack Johnson and Jack Dempsey."

Johnson, in fact, did face Langford once. Johnson was twenty-eight years old at the time, in his fighting prime, but not yet heavyweight champ. Langford was only twenty, and was more than forty pounds lighter than Johnson. Johnson won the fight convincingly (Langford described it as "the only real beating I ever took"), but couldn't knock Langford out. He got a full taste of just how tough Langford was and how hard he could hit.

DID YOU KNOW?

- Langford spent the bulk of his boxing career fighting in and around Boston, earning him such nicknames as "The Boston Terror" and "The Boston Tar Baby."

- Langford fought in five different weight classes during his career: lightweight, welterweight, middleweight, light heavyweight, and heavyweight. He started his career at 135 pounds, and finished at approximately 185 pounds.

- It is believed that, off the record, Langford fought between 500 and 600 bouts in his lifetime.

- Of his 252 recorded professional fights, Langford had 99 knockout wins.

Johnson later became World heavyweight champion, but he would never agree to give Langford a rematch. Publicly, Johnson claimed that no one would pay to see two Black men fight for the title. Privately, he admitted fear that Langford would take his belt.

"He's got a chance to win against anyone in the world," said Johnson. "I'm the first Black champion and I'm going to be the last!"

Langford took part in 252 recorded professional fights in a career that lasted from 1902 to 1926. He never won a world title at any weight. He defeated lightweight champ Joe Gans in 1903, but was denied the title because he came into the fight two pounds over the weight limit. Nine months later, he fought Joe Walcott, the reigning

World welterweight champ. That bout ended in a draw, although most in attendance felt Langford had achieved clear victory. He would never receive another chance to fight for a World title.

Denied this opportunity, Langford was forced to repeatedly fight the same opponents over and over again. They were mostly fellow outstanding Black boxers who, like Langford, were denied title shots by the colour barrier. When he did fight white opponents, he was frequently asked to carry them (as described above), which he knew he had to do if he wanted to keep getting fights.

In June of 1917, Langford was injured during a fight, suffering damage that left him blind in his left eye. And yet he fought on. In 1922, at the probable age of thirty-seven, he scored a second-round knockout of future middleweight champ Tiger Flowers, despite an injury that all but blinded his remaining good eye. And still he fought on for another two years, winning fights on instinct and genius.

"He was such a brilliant fighter," says Silver. "He could fight on the inside for the entire fight, and he would instinctively know from his years of experience where his opponents' arms were and so forth. He was blind, but he could still win fights!"

Eventually, though, Langford could no longer disguise his ailment, and after he walked to the wrong corner during a fight in 1926, his licence was revoked and he retired.

By 1944, Langford was all but forgotten and living penniless and destitute in Harlem. He was a source of fascination for Al Laney, a reporter from the *New York Herald Tribune*, who made it a mission to find this great boxer who had seemingly vanished from the earth. After months of searching, Laney tracked him down and featured Langford

SAM LANGFORD

in a series of short stories. Laney also helped establish a sportswriters' fund that cared for Langford and allowed him to live comfortably through his remaining years.

In 1952, Langford moved back to Boston and quietly lived out his life in a private nursing home. He passed away on January 12, 1956, at the approximate age of seventy, and only ten weeks after being named to the Boxing Hall of Fame.

More than sixty years later, he is regularly listed by *Ring Magazine* as one of Top 10 boxers to have ever lived. Sam Langford was simply that good.

15 SMALL-TOWN HOMETOWN HEROES

1 **Richard Beazley**: Hantsport, Hants County, track and field, original inductee.

2 **Kevin Dugas**: Little Brook Station, Digby County, golf, inducted 2014.

3 **Scott Fraser**: Shubenacadie, Colchester County, stock car racing, inducted 2014.

4 **Jimmy Gray**: Joggins Mines, Cumberland County, baseball and hockey, inducted 1981.

5 **Fred Lake**: Cornwallis, Annapolis County, baseball, inducted 2007.

6 **Penny LaRocque**: Yarmouth, Yarmouth County, curling, inducted 2007.

7 **Lowell MacDonald**: Thorburn, Pictou County, hockey, inducted 1982.

8 **Donald MacVicar**: Donkin, Cape Breton County, powerlifting, inducted 2001.

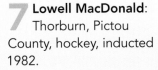

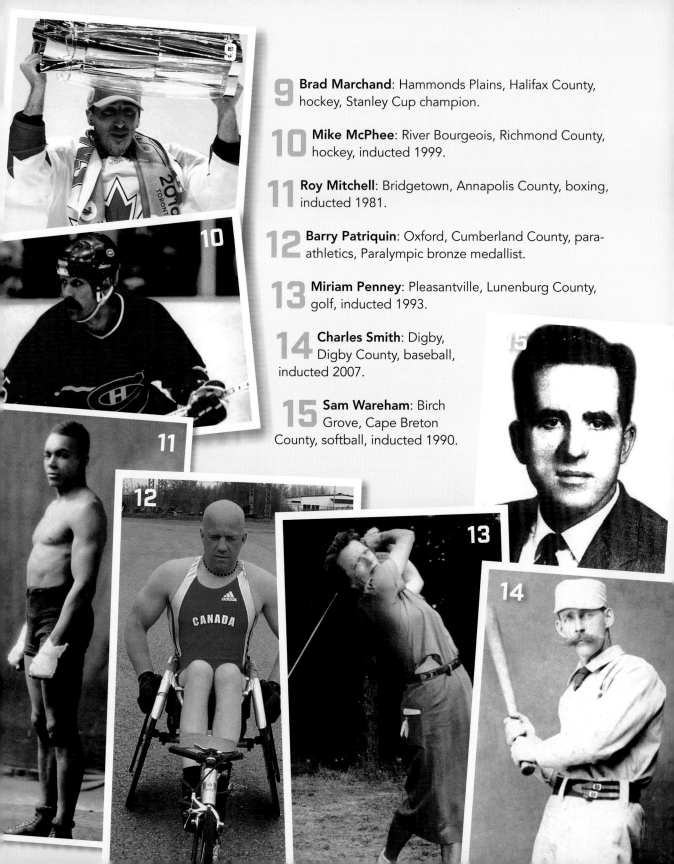

9 **Brad Marchand**: Hammonds Plains, Halifax County, hockey, Stanley Cup champion.

10 **Mike McPhee**: River Bourgeois, Richmond County, hockey, inducted 1999.

11 **Roy Mitchell**: Bridgetown, Annapolis County, boxing, inducted 1981.

12 **Barry Patriquin**: Oxford, Cumberland County, para-athletics, Paralympic bronze medallist.

13 **Miriam Penney**: Pleasantville, Lunenburg County, golf, inducted 1993.

14 **Charles Smith**: Digby, Digby County, baseball, inducted 2007.

15 **Sam Wareham**: Birch Grove, Cape Breton County, softball, inducted 1990.

NANCY GARAPICK

Halifax, Swimming, Inducted 1986

By Joel Jacobson

How could an unknown thirteen-year-old girl from Halifax, Nova Scotia, set a world swimming record? "Impossible," people said.

It was April 29, 1975, at the Eastern Canadian Championships in London, Ontario, that Nancy Garapick proved it was possible when she established a new world standard in the 200-metre backstroke. Her time of 2:16.33 was 1 second better than the previous mark.

One month later, Garapick raced to gold in the 100-metre and 200-metre backstroke events at the Canadian Championships in Winnipeg. In July, Garapick won silver in the 200-metre backstroke, and bronze in the 100-metre backstroke at the World Aquatic Championships in Cali, Colombia.

Now people knew who Nancy Garapick was.

Take a step back for a moment to the build-up to Cali.

This bubbling thirteen-year-old kid was living the moment, having the time of her life. And the stats were there, the record, the winning times, but numbers don't measure heart or indomitable spirit and joy.

Garapick was the best story of those Games. In four months, she had climbed from thirty-eighth in the world to the world record holder. She was told, every day, she was the only hope Canada had against the power of the East Germans.

At the start of the 100-metre backstroke final, she lined up against Ulrike Richter, world champion at 100 metres, and Birgit Treiber, who had taken back the world 200-metre record. The towering, muscular representatives of East Germany dwarfed the 113-pound Garapick. The finish? Richter, Treiber, and Garapick for gold, silver and bronze.

Garapick felt more confident about the 200-metre distance, having never considered herself a sprinter. However, when asked by the media for her thoughts entering the race, she admitted that she felt the pressure of all of Canada wanting her to win.

Garapick ended up breaking the world 200-metre backstroke record, but her achievement was overshadowed by the fact that Treiber also broke it, moving ahead of Garapick in the last few strokes to win the race. Treiber clocked 2:15.46 and Garapick 2:16.09. That's only 63/100ths of a second between gold and silver. However, Garapick had now caught the attention of the world and let everyone know that the young kid from Halifax was just starting her domination in the pool.

Garapick may have been setting world records, taking questions at press conferences, and competing under immense pressure, but she

DID YOU KNOW?

- Garapick is a record holder in the NCAA 200-metre freestyle.

- Garapick holds a Bachelor of Arts from Dalhousie University and a Bachelor of Education from Mount St. Vincent University.

- Garapick's achievements have been recognized by the Nova Scotia Sport Hall of Fame (1986), the Canadian Olympic Hall of Fame (1993), and Canada's Sports Hall of Fame (2008).

- Garapick was the youngest athlete to ever be named Canada's Female Athlete of the Year.

was still only a young kid, and sports columnist Jim Taylor recalls how she ran to coach Nigel Kemp at the end of those championships in Cali with visible disappointment.

Taylor writes that Garapick apologized to Kemp for not winning gold, but Kemp simply replied, "Sunshine, you did just fine."

Her amazing four-month run of successes was more than just fine and earned her the title of Canada's Female Athlete of the Year in 1975.

A swimming veteran at fourteen, Garapick was one of Canada's brightest medal hopefuls at the 1976 Summer Olympics in Montreal.

Garapick captured two bronze medals in the 100- and 200-metre backstroke events behind Richter and Treiber. The East German team was widely viewed as users of performance-enhancing drugs.

Many years later those suspicions were confirmed, but the International Olympic Committee chose not to pursue the matter or take away the East Germans' medals.

Legendary Halifax swim coach Kemp had a poolside seat for much of Garapick's career, including the 1976 Olympics.

"Nancy has always regarded her Olympic experiences as a moment in time from a historical perspective," says Kemp, a member of the Nova Scotia Sport Hall of Fame. "She believes that she did all she possibly could from both a racing and preparation perspective and that is what the medals she earned represent to her."

Kemp continues: "We suspected then, and certainly know now, that the East Germans were using performance-enhancing drugs. FINA and the IOC have chosen not to revisit this specific situation, either through the re-awarding of medals or noting the East German performances were aided."

The expectations for Garapick at the 1976 Olympics were unbelievably high for such a young athlete and Kemp helped her keep things in perspective.

In 1968, expectations for Canadian Olympian Elaine Tanner had been high and silver medal–winning swims were regarded as disappointments.

"As a consequence, I tried to keep a cap on Nancy's media exposure and hold expectations in check," Kemp says. "It was an attempt to manage the pressure she had to deal with."

Garapick continued to win medals on the world scene, capturing a bronze (4x100-metre freestyle relay) at the 1978 World Championships in Berlin. She then dominated the 1979 Pan American Games in San Juan, with two silver and three bronze medals.

Garapick missed the 1980 Olympics in Moscow when Canada joined a US-led boycott but continued a nine-year stretch as a member of the Canadian national team through 1983.

By then, she had spent a few years on the University of Southern California swim team, which she followed by studying at Dalhousie University where she set several AUS and USPORTS records as a

TAKE THEIR WORD FOR IT

A slender and well-streamlined swimmer, she presented relatively minimal resistance in the water. And as a physically mature athlete, I believe that her body weight-to-strength ratio was advantageous when combined with factors such as her excellent stroke technique and positive mental approach.

—Nigel Kemp, Hall of Famer and Garapick's former coach

member of the Dal Tigers swim team under Coach Kemp.

Garapick's competitive swimming career came to an end in 1983.

Now living quietly in British Columbia, where she was a school-teacher for many years, Garapick has a resume to be envied: she established seventy-nine provincial records, won thirty-eight Canadian Championship medals, seventeen National titles and of course, the two Olympic bronze medals. Many of her provincial bests are still being chased by Nova Scotia's up-and-coming swimmers.

And, when her name is mentioned today, *everyone* knows who Nancy Garapick is and what she accomplished.

NANCY GARAPICK

15 GREAT ATLANTIC UNIVERSITY ATHLETES FROM NOVA SCOTIA SCHOOLS

1 **Andrew Cole at Dalhousie**: eleven-time AUAA swimming champion, two-time CIAU champion, All-Canadian for four straight years.

2 **Malcolm Davis at Saint Mary's**: All-Canadian hockey player (1978) with SMU, played 100 games in the NHL.

3 **Chris Flynn at Saint Mary's**: As SMU football quarterback, was named the nation's outstanding player a record three consecutive seasons; threw 87 career touchdown passes, which remains a CIAU record; led SMU to four AUAA titles and two wins in the Atlantic Bowl.

4 **Mickey Fox at Saint Mary's**: four-time All-Canadian basketball star, two-time MVP of the National Championship tournament. In 1979, set a three-game National Championship scoring mark of 101 points, a record that still stands to this day.

5 **Eric Gillis at St. Francis Xavier**: track and field standout. CIS cross-country champion in 2003, four-time All-Canadian, two-time St. FX Male Athlete of the Year, three-time Olympian.

6 **John Hatch at St. Francis Xavier**: all-time leading scorer in St. FX men's basketball history, three-time AUAA MVP, three-time first team All-Canadian; represented Canada at the 1984 and 1988 Olympics.

7 **Brian Heaney at Acadia**: two-time All-Canadian basketball player. Scored 74 points in one game against Mount Allison, a national record that still stands; also won three titles as a coach of the Saint Mary's Huskies. He is the only AUS player to play in the NBA.

8 Theresa MacCuish at St. Francis Xavier: all-time leading scorer in St. FX women's basketball history, AUS and CIS Rookie of the Year, five-time AUS All-Star, two-time All-Canadian, four-time St. FX Female Athlete of the Year.

9 Karin Maessen at Dalhousie: three-time All-Canadian volleyball player, named CIAU national player of the year in 1982; member of the Canadian national team for nine years; Nova Scotia Female Athlete of the Year in 1981 and 1982.

10 Suzanne Muir at Saint Mary's: two-time women's AUAA soccer MVP and 1992 CIAU tournament All-Star.

11 William Njoku at Saint Mary's: second leading scorer in SMU basketball history, AUS MVP in 1993 and 1994, CIS Player of the Year in 1994, member of the Canadian national team for ten years; drafted in the second round of the 1994 NBA draft.

12 David Sharpe at Dalhousie: four-time AUS male swimmer of the year, Olympian at the 2012 Games, winner of thirteen CIS medals.

13 Cindy Tye at Acadia: AUS soccer Rookie of the Year in 1990, AUS All-Star 1991–95, CIS All-Canadian 1994–95, member of the Canadian national team in 2001 and 2002.

14 Ted Upshaw at Acadia: member of the 1977 Acadia national championship basketball team. In 1981, led the nation in both scoring (29 ppg) and rebounding (10 rpg), AUAA MVP in 1981, CIAU All-Canadian in 1981.

15 Ross Webb at Saint Mary's: soccer standout. Scored 72 goals in his five-year university career, which remains a CIAU record; won the AUAA scoring title in each of his five years; won CIAU Rookie of the Year and was named All-Canadian four times.

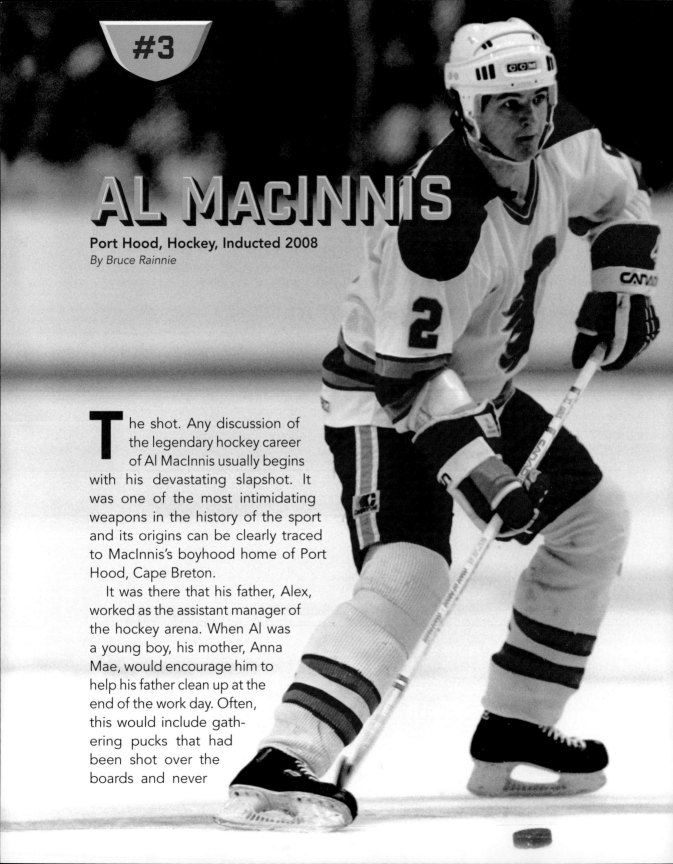

AL MacINNIS

Port Hood, Hockey, Inducted 2008
By Bruce Rainnie

The shot. Any discussion of the legendary hockey career of Al MacInnis usually begins with his devastating slapshot. It was one of the most intimidating weapons in the history of the sport and its origins can be clearly traced to MacInnis's boyhood home of Port Hood, Cape Breton.

It was there that his father, Alex, worked as the assistant manager of the hockey arena. When Al was a young boy, his mother, Anna Mae, would encourage him to help his father clean up at the end of the work day. Often, this would include gathering pucks that had been shot over the boards and never retrieved. Needless to say, by the end of the hockey season, young Al would have quite the collection.

"I was never much of a beach guy," MacInnis would say years later. "But I loved, absolutely loved, shooting these pucks at some plywood that was leaning against my father's barn. Every day for hours I would shoot, to the point where my hands would sometimes be blistered. But that was how I liked to spend my summers!"

Turns out it was time very well spent. That shot would help Al play at the highest levels of minor hockey, but mostly as a right-winger. That would change, though, when Donnie MacIsaac of Antigonish, coach of the Nova AAA Midgets, made a move that would alter the course of MacInnis's hockey career.

TAKE THEIR WORD FOR IT

Al was just so good for so long. I think most hockey people would say that Bobby Orr, Nicklas Lidstrom, Doug Harvey, Ray Bourque, and Denis Potvin, in some order, are the five best defencemen ever. But Al is definitely in the next tier, and not too far behind that top five. His shot was probably the greatest power-play weapon the game has ever seen, his passing was sublime, and he became an exceptionally good defender. He was also an awesome teammate. Not too many players are revered in two cities, but Al was just that sort of guy.

—Ron MacLean, Host of *Hockey Night in Canada*

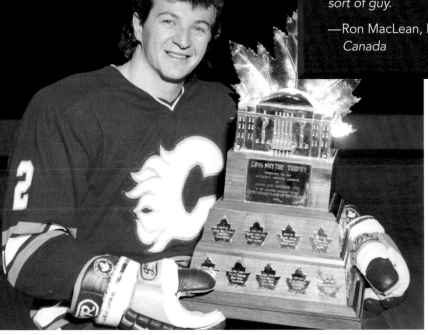

AL
MacINNIS

"He didn't think I was a good enough skater to play forward, and he was right," MacInnis recalls with a laugh. "But he liked my hockey sense, my passing ability, and he *loved* my shot, so he put me back on right defence. Smart guy, that Donnie MacIsaac!"

His new position agreed with him immediately, and MacInnis went on to a sparkling junior career with the Kitchener Rangers of the OHL. He was twice a First Team All-Star, was named the league's top defenceman in 1983, and tied Bobby Orr's league record for goals by a defenceman in one season (thirty-eight). He also set a Canadian Hockey League record by scoring five goals in a game as a defenceman. Al MacInnis and his booming shot were ready for the National Hockey League.

He joined the Calgary Flames full-time in 1983 and wasted little time in launching his legend. In a game in St. Louis in January 1984, MacInnis picked up a puck near centre ice and, a few strides later, drew back his stick, and leaned into one.

"I really got a hold of it," MacInnis says. "It took off kind of like a golf ball."

The puck exploded up high and tight on Blues goalie Mike Liut, and hit him squarely in the mask. The mask cracked, Liut toppled, and the puck magically fell into the net. The episode left fans startled, and the goalie spellbound.

"There's hard, and then there's Al MacInnis hard," Liut would say after the game. "If that happens too often, you have to sit down and re-evaluate what you're doing with your life."

Liut wasn't the only goaltender mesmerized by the MacInnis missile. During the 1989 Stanley Cup Final versus the Montreal

Canadiens, MacInnis scored four goals in a Flames six-game series win. He won the Conn Smythe Trophy as playoff MVP, and clearly had the better of Hall of Fame goalie Patrick Roy. So much so, in fact, that after the series, long-time Flames executive and Sydney native Al MacNeil offered the following:

MacInnis just about terrorized Roy. He had him worried, bad, because of the howitzer. No doubt about it. That was an edge we had. When you have a guy like Al, it gives you such an advantage. He was a scary guy with that slapshot.

DID YOU KNOW?

- Al MacInnis is the only player from Nova Scotia ever to be inducted into the Hockey Hall of Fame.

- MacInnis has been a generous supporter of his home community. He committed $100,000 to arena renovations in Port Hood (the arena is now known as the Al MacInnis Sports Centre), and, on the day he was inducted into the Nova Scotia Sport Hall of Fame, he donated $100,000 to the Inverness County Memorial Hospital in memory of his parents.

- At the NHL All-Star Game Skills Competition, Al MacInnis won the "Hardest Shot Contest" a record seven times!

- Al MacInnis ranks third all-time in points by a defenceman with 1,274. Only Ray Bourque and Paul Coffey had more.

- MacInnis is one of only five defencemen to score 100 points in a season. The others? Bobby Orr, Paul Coffey, Brian Leetch, and Denis Potvin.

- A two-time Olympian, MacInnis played for Team Canada in the 1998 and 2002 Games.

- Individual Awards Won:
  - Max Kaminsky Trophy (OHL top defenceman) – 1981
  - Conn Smythe Trophy (NHL Playoff MVP) – 1989
  - Norris Trophy (NHL top defenceman) – 1999

- Team Awards Won:
  - Memorial Cup – 1982
  - Stanley Cup – 1989
  - Canada Cup – 1991
  - Olympic Gold Medal – 2002

MacInnis would star with the Flames until 1994, before moving on to play the next decade with the St. Louis Blues. Although he never won a Stanley Cup with the Blues, he continued to play at an extraordinary level late into his career, winning his only Norris Trophy as the league's top defenceman at age thirty-five.

"To be honest, I thought I would never win one of those," MacInnis says. "Look at the guys who played in my era—Bourque, Coffey, Chelios. They were all better than me. But I always stayed in really good shape, and when I finally won the Norris, I think I was probably playing the best all-around hockey of my career. Persistence pays off I guess!"

Persistence and total dedication to your craft. Al MacInnis played a remarkable twenty-three years in the National Hockey League and retired as one of the finest defencemen to ever lace up a pair of skates. Following his retirement, Al, his wife, Jackie, and their four children settled in St. Louis. In 2006, Al was named the Blues's vice-president of hockey operations—it's a position he holds to this day.

The shot helped make his name, but commitment helped shape his game. Number two sits at number three on the list of the fifteen greatest athletes in the history of Nova Scotia. The pride of Port Hood—Al MacInnis.

THE FIRST 15 NOVA SCOTIAN NHL PLAYERS

1 **Lester Lowther of Amherst**: played first game in 1914 with Toronto St. Pats, original inductee.

2 **Mickey Roach of Glace Bay**: played first game in 1919 with Toronto St. Pats, original inductee.

3 **Bill Stuart of Amherst**: played first game in 1920 with Toronto St. Pats, original inductee.

4 **Stanton Jackson of Parrsboro**: played first game in 1921 with Toronto St. Pats, original inductee.

5 **Pat Nolan of Glace Bay**: played first game in 1921 with Toronto St. Pats.

6 **Ted Stackhouse of Wolfville**: played first game in 1921 with Toronto St. Pats, original inductee.

7 **Charles Fraser of Stellarton**: played first game in 1923 with Hamilton Tigers.

8 **John Ingram of Halifax**: played first game in 1924 with Boston Bruins.

9 **John McKinnon of Guysborough**: played first game in 1925 with Montreal Canadiens.

10 **Gord Kuhn of Truro**: played first game in 1932 with New York Americans, original inductee.

11 **William Hollett of North Sydney**: played first game in 1933 with Toronto Maple Leafs.

12 **Claude Bourque of Oxford**: played first game in 1938 with Montreal Canadiens.

13 **Irv McGibbon of Antigonish**: played first game in 1942 with Montreal Canadiens.

14 **Wally Wilson of Berwick**: played first game in 1947 with Boston Bruins.

15 **Bert Hirschfeld of Halifax**: played first game in 1949 with Montreal Canadiens, inducted 1980.

COLLEEN JONES

Halifax, Curling, Inducted 2011

By Joel Jacobson

Tenacity. Self-trust. Competitiveness. Leadership. Work ethic. Longevity.

And, above all, a winner.

That's what makes Colleen Jones one of the best athletes Nova Scotia has ever produced.

Halifax-born and raised, this phenomenal curler has set standards that will live for a long time in the province and even in Canada.

After her first provincial win in 1978, and, even more so, following her first

Canadian championship at the Scotties in 1982, Jones and her teams had targets on their backs. That never bothered them, particularly after they started a string of five Scotties wins in six years between 1999 and 2004, the last four in succession. World titles in 2001 and 2004 and silver in 2003 enhanced their glorious record.

Jones reflects on her beginnings in curling: "I went to the rink with my older sisters when I was young and loved hanging out and being social. After a couple of years, the sport seemed easy and I wanted more. In 1976, we went to Junior Nationals, and didn't do very well, but that was a taste at that level and I wanted more of that, too."

Jones was only nineteen in 1978 when she skipped the first of her sixteen Nova Scotia champion women's teams. A year later, she won silver with Nova Scotia at the Canada Games in Brandon, Manitoba.

In 1982, in her second of twenty-one appearances at the Scotties, she became the youngest ever to win a women's Canadian title.

She wouldn't win another until 1999, when her most dominant team fell into place. Second stone Mary-Anne Arsenault became the final piece of the puzzle. Vice-skip Kim Kelly had been with Jones since 1989. Nancy Delahunt, lead, and Jones had been friends and teammates for years.

Remarking on how the quartet had a chemistry together, Delahunt says: "The three of us brought out the best in Colleen. I've never met anyone with a more insatiable appetite for winning than Colleen, but for her to be the best, she had to be comfortable with us—and she was."

Delahunt adds, "There was no other Colleen Jones. I never saw anyone across the country like her. She taught us how to win and what it means to win."

"We were all competitive," says Kelly. "But Colleen taught us how to compete with the belief we can win. She was the boss, too. She looked after the logistics, how to get ready to play, how to practise. Yet she trusted us to train on our own but needed accountability that we were putting in the work. Her mantra was, 'I'm all in (to win). You'd better come along.'"

Kelly says Jones never rested on her laurels, almost to a fault.

"After a win, she'd be happy for maybe sixteen hours. Then she'd wake up and say 'What

can we do better?' Even after winning a Worlds she'd say, 'We were lucky. We need to do this or that to win again.'"

The teammates trusted their leader implicitly. Kelly says other players would call them "puppets" but they'd retort, "You don't get it. You don't understand the trust we have in Colleen and what she believes we can do, too."

"Their work ethic was unmatched," says coach/psychologist Ken Bagnell who was with the Jones foursome from 2001 to 2005. Alternates Laine Peters, Mary Sue Radford, and Coach Peter Corkum also helped ensure success through the years. "The amount of work, the amount of practice, set the bar for what people today do in curling and in sport all over the world.

Jones admits that she practised a lot, probably more than anyone else, and that built the confidence that she could make whatever shot faced her.

Kelly says Jones's major strength was her ability in the clutch. "Even if she wasn't playing well, she'd make what she needed to. On a must-make shot, she could focus and be perfect."

Jones was also a pioneer in making physical fitness part of curling, being an athlete rather than someone who just threw rocks and did some sweeping. She was dedicated and ensured her teammates worked out, trained, and watched their diet. And they threw thousands of practice rocks so they were ready for game situations.

The competitive juices continue to flow. Still curling at a high level, Jones and her team of Kelly, Mary Sue Radford, and Delahunt captured the 2017 World Senior Championship in Lethbridge, Alberta, after winning the Canadian title in Digby, Nova Scotia, in 2016.

Jones also owns a pair of Canadian mixed curling championships, winning in 1993 in Swift Current and 1999 in Victoria.

Thirteen years after winning Worlds in 2004, Jones says the sensation of winning a Senior World title was just as special.

TAKE THEIR WORD FOR IT

I have so much respect for Colleen Jones and what she was able to accomplish. She was such a great competitor and left no stone unturned when it came to preparation. Her team was always the fittest, both physically and mentally. In fact, the work she did in sport psychology was ground-breaking. Nobody else was doing it at the time, but everyone is doing it now. She's a pioneer, a legend, and on a short list of best skips ever.

—Jennifer Jones, five-time Scotties champion and the 2014 Olympic Gold Medallist

"Winning is winning. Whenever you win something this big, the euphoria is the exact same," she says. "You want to hold onto that feeling forever. Winning at this age is maybe sweeter than when I won at twenty-one or thirty-nine because your body's aging. There's a lot more work to maintain your ability and talent at this age. You have to keep improving your game."

Jones, a member of the Nova Scotia Sport Hall of Fame, Canada's Sports Hall of Fame, and the Canadian Curling Hall of Fame, says she'll continue to chase National and World championships. "I think I have a lot left in my tank. I think the girls embrace the challenge to get better as much as I do, that they're renewed and re-energized. It's a wonderful goal to have at any age, and especially our age."

She admits that win-at-all-costs attitude is, thankfully, no longer there.

"Still, when I step on the ice, something goes through my veins. It's showtime. When you've spent over forty years chasing something, it never leaves you."

COLLEEN JONES

15 MORE NAMES YOU SHOULD KNOW IN NOVA SCOTIA SPORT

1 **Freddie Cameron**: winner of the Boston Marathon in 1910 (despite having never before run a distance longer than ten miles), original inductee.

2 **Edna Lockhart Duncanson**: player with New York Bloomer Girls baseball team and Staten Island Shamrocks semi-pro basketball team in the 1930s, inducted 1996.

3 **David Fraser**: founder of the Nova Scotia Blind Sports Association, inducted 2008.

4 **John Giovannetti**: two-time Canadian trap shooting champion despite losing his left arm in the Second World War, inducted 2006.

5 **Bill Hannon**: outstanding hockey, baseball, and softball player who was drafted to the New York Rovers EAHL team, inducted 2000.

6 **Lloyd Heisler and Russell Langille (dory racing team)**: holder of Gloucester and Lunenburg International Dory Racing titles between 1952 and 1955, inducted 1982.

7 **Charles "Tiny" Hermann**: Grey Cup champion who helped introduce Canadian football to the Maritimes, original inductee.

8 **Maisie Howard:** winner of numerous Nova Scotia, Maritime, and Canadian golfing titles between ages seventeen and twenty in the 1930s, inducted 1982.

9 **Josephine Laba**: Junior Canadian champion in four track and field events, inducted 1995.

10 **Con Olson**: winner of 189 of 208 distance races and ran across Canso Causeway when it opened, original inductee.

11 **Arnie Patterson**: radio personality on CJCH and CFDR covering hockey and baseball, inducted 2008.

12 **Burns Wesley Pierce**: cyclist who covered 1,732 miles in a six-day endurance race, original inductee.

13 **Phil Scott**: nine-time World logrolling champion, inducted 1987.

14 **Paul Tingley**: five-time Paralympian (2000, 2004, 2008, 2012, and 2016) with one gold medal and two bronze in sailing.

15 **Terrance "Tiger" Warrington**: Canadian light-heavyweight boxing champion and Canadian heavyweight champion, original inductee.

SIDNEY CROSBY

Cole Harbour, Hockey

By Bruce Rainnie

The *Boston Globe* used to have a columnist by the name of George Frazier. He was a tremendous talent whose writing was laden with style, colour, and acerbic wit. He wrote often of something he called *duende*. When asked to define it, he struggled but settled on "that certain something that sets persons apart. It might be 'soul,' but it might also be 'star quality. 'It is a power that transmits a profound feeling from the heart of the artist to his audience with the minimum of fuss and the maximum of restraint."

Frazier first sensed and wrote of *duende* when he first saw Joe DiMaggio grace an outfield. It wasn't merely greatness that he saw, nor majesty, nor aura. It was *duende*, and he had to learn more about it. "To say that *duende* is simply charisma or panache or flair is rather to demean it," Frazier wrote, "for while it is certainly all those things, it is the nth power of them. It is chemistry."

Which brings me to the subject of this chapter—the Number One athlete in Nova Scotia history, Sidney Patrick Crosby of Cole Harbour, Nova Scotia.

I've found myself thinking a lot these past few years about what Mr. Frazier would think of young Mr. Crosby. I feel fairly safe in saying he would find Sidney overflowing with *duende*. In fact, he would probably write that he oozes it. And he'd be bang on.

I've had the privilege of working as a rink-side reporter for close to 150 NHL games over the last decade. Many of those games have featured Sidney Crosby and the Pittsburgh Penguins. Let me assure you, when Crosby and the Pens come to town, it brings a totally different ambience to the arena.

For example, at a typical Saturday night game in Toronto (say between the Leafs and the Sabres), teams take to the ice at 6:30 sharp for a pre-game skate. Generally at this time, the stands are about two-thirds empty and gradually fill to capacity by the time the puck is dropped at 7:10 P.M. But when Pittsburgh is in Toronto, you look around at 6:30 and realize that 95 percent of the fans have already arrived. And man, are they pumped! So many flashbulbs are going off that you'd swear a massive lightning storm was taking place inside the arena. Every male fan, no matter the age, looks downright giddy. Every female fan, no matter the age, looks like she spent an extra fifteen minutes getting ready. Little kids press their freckled faces

TAKE THEIR WORD FOR IT

"It has been amazing to watch him become the man that he is today. He's an incredible person. He does so much on the ice, but also off the ice with his foundation in Nova Scotia. He's a great young man and I love having him around."

—Mario Lemieux, Hockey Hall of Fame inductee, one of the "100 Greatest NHL Players," and owner of the Pittsburgh Penguins

SIDNEY CROSBY

against the Plexiglas, pens, programs, and photos clutched in their anxious fingers, hoping that Crosby will suddenly abandon warm-up, leave the ice, and jump into the stands to start signing. It's a wondrous thing to witness up close, and it has to be the very definition of *duende*. And the amazing thing is that this kid has had it since he was, well, a kid.

I go back a long way with Crosby. I first heard of him in 1995, when I was working as the late-night sports anchor for the CBC in Halifax. I kept getting calls from people in Cole Harbour. Over and over I was told that I had to come do a profile on this eight-year old hockey phenomenon who was setting scoring records while playing against boys two and three years older. "How good could he really be?" I wondered.

Skeptical, but admittedly curious, I finally relented and headed one evening to Cole Harbour Place (the local arena) to watch Crosby play. What I saw stunned me. For one thing, the stands were filled to capacity for a minor hockey game. There must have been close to one thousand people there to watch this kid play. And what a show he put on! If memory serves, the Cole Harbour Red Wings beat Shearwater that night by a score of 9 to 4, with Crosby, by far the youngest player on the ice, scoring four goals and adding four assists. I vividly recall

thinking that this was the best young hockey player I had ever seen. It was crystal clear even then (yes, at age eight) that if he grew to a sufficient size and maintained what was an obvious love for the game, professional hockey stardom was inevitable.

Fast forward a few years to the 2002 edition of CBC's *Hockey Day in Canada*. The producers of the show called me a few months prior to the broadcast looking for a catchy hockey story from Nova Scotia. I suggested a feature on Crosby. He was fourteen by this time and playing with young men two to three years older on the Dartmouth Midget AAA Subways. He was smack dab in the middle of a season that would see him score ninety-five goals and ninety-eight assists in just seventy-four games and lead his team to second place nationally at the Air Canada Cup.

Still though, the producers were hesitant, saying, "We don't like to focus too much on young players—so many of them never pan out." To which I responded, "You *have* to let me do this story—I guarantee you that in five years this kid will be the best hockey player in the world."

"He's from where again?" they asked.

"Cole Harbour," I replied.

"Not exactly a hotbed, Bruce."

"Guys, you have to trust me."

Eventually, to their credit, they did.

We met for our first extended interview in December of 2001. My cameraman and I paid a visit to the Crosby family home on what would become a memorable Sunday afternoon. After meeting his parents, Trina and Troy, and his sister, Taylor, our next order of business became trying to figure out where to shoot some footage and interview Crosby. That mystery was instantly solved, however, when we saw the basement.

SIDNEY CROSBY

In one room, Troy had created a scaled-down, makeshift offensive zone, complete with red and blue lines on the concrete floor and a regulation-size net for Crosby to aim pucks at. About ten feet or so behind the net and positioned off to the side was what has become arguably this country's most famous appliance—the Crosby family dryer (now

on display, by the way, at the Nova Scotia Sport Hall of Fame). This poor thing was a total dog's breakfast, the victim of too many pucks shot with force, but just wide of the goal, by young Sidney. There were dials and buttons missing everywhere, and dents and black puck marks all over. Miraculously, though, it still worked! For the feature, we had Crosby fire puck after puck into the net and then, with his last shot, deliberately miss and further add to the woes of the dryer. As the noise of puck on metal filled the house, the sheepish look on his face was priceless.

The family room made up the other part of the basement, and it was brimming with trophies and press clippings Crosby had accumulated in his still-blossoming hockey career. It provided the perfect backdrop for our all-important first interview with Crosby. As we focused the camera on his whiskerless face, I directed my first ever in-depth question to the young man, and I remember it vividly:

"Sidney, when did you know, when did you first sense, that you were a better-than-average hockey player?"

In a voice that was still an octave or two away from full maturity, the answer came back with the mix of self-assurance and humility that would eventually define him: "Well, I remember when I was in novice, I scored 169 goals in 20 games, and I realized then that I might have somewhat of a scoring touch."

Isn't that beautiful? People often ask me what Crosby is really like, and my answer is always the same: just watch how he signs autographs, especially for kids. You can see his true colours. So many professional athletes just scribble their names by rote, never looking up, never personalizing the experience for the fan. Crosby is the exact

opposite—he always makes eye contact, always engages in a bit of conversation, and always goes out of his way to make sure a little kid leaves with a smile. *Duende*....

You wonder where this decency comes from only as long as it takes for you to have a lengthy conversation with his parents. Trina and Troy are two of the most grounded, least demonstrative, least spotlight-seeking people you'd ever want to meet. They have rock-solid values and a real handle on what is truly essential in life. I know from an early age they taught Sidney that "please" and "thank you" were as fundamental as stickhandling and skating; that looking someone in the eye when having a conversation was as meaningful as an overtime goal; that remembering your sister's birthday was as important as any MVP award. Crosby learned these lessons well, and he's clearly never for-

gotten them. In every character-defining way, he's exactly the same today as he was before money and acclaim entered his life. That's quite a compliment to him *and* his mom and dad.

Before moving on, one other thing is worth noting regarding Crosby's parents. We live in an age where there are myriad stories of overbearing parents who pushed or forced their kids into a sport, and perhaps robbed them of some childhood along the way (tennis dads seem to be particular culprits). I can tell you unequivocally that Trina and Troy *never* pushed Crosby. If anything, he pushed them! So hard, in fact, that they were often extended to their financial limits trying to keep up. Missed bill payments, extra jobs late at night—these were facts of life for the Crosbys, all to make sure their son had good, protective gear and the opportunity to travel to tournaments or attend camps in the summer. They afforded him every chance to follow his dream and fulfill the potential he showed at such a young age. But they never steered or forced him.

My most memorable experience with Crosby came in December of 2002, when cameraman

Eric Woolliscroft and I were dispatched by *Hockey Night in Canada* (the producers had become believers by then) to Faribault, Minnesota, where Crosby was spending his grade 10 year at a prep school called Shattuck St. Mary's. Shattuck had heavily recruited Crosby, wanting him to be the crown jewel in the school's renowned hockey program. Woolliscroft and I arrived, tasked with preparing a five-minute feature on Crosby to air on a future edition of *Hockey Night in Canada.*

We met up with Crosby, pinned a microphone on his shirt, and followed him to his first class, which was French. When it came his turn to speak, Crosby looked at the teacher and said, "Je suis Canadien!" As his classmates giggled, Crosby then spun in his seat to give a spirited thumbs-up to Woolliscroft's camera. Hey, it never hurts when the subject of your profile is a little bit of a ham!

After the school day ended, we headed to the small rink on campus to watch the Shattuck team practice. On the ice that day were future Buffalo Sabre Drew Stafford, future Tampa Bay Lightning Matt Smaby, and future Los Angeles King Jack Johnson. The squad was loaded, and would later go on to win the US National Championship. Still, though, one player clearly stood out above the rest. I remember saying to Woolliscroft that day, "You know, if an alien landed right now from Mars and knew nothing about hockey, I bet you it would take him less than five minutes to pick out the best player on the ice." It was that obvious.

When practice ended, we walked with Crosby back to his dorm and prepared to say our goodbyes for the night. Before that could happen though, Crosby asked, "What are you guys doing now?" I replied that we were probably going to drive to Bloomington, get some dinner, and then go visit the Mall of America. Seeing a wistful look suddenly fall over his face, I hesitantly followed with, "You wanna come with us?" The "yes" was out of his mouth faster than a speeding photon!

SIDNEY
CROSBY

So we all piled into our rented minivan and began what I remember to be about a forty-five-minute drive to Bloomington.

A spectacular Italian dinner preceded our visit to the second biggest mall in North America. Woolliscroft went one way to do some shopping for his wife while Crosby and I went the other way just to browse around. We eventually came to a little cafe area, grabbed a couple of fruit smoothies, and sat for what I thought would be a minute or two. That minute quickly became an hour as we people-watched and talked. Eventually, as you would expect, the conversation drifted to sports. Crosby was fascinated as I told him stories of famous athletes and their intense drive. He was particularly transfixed by a bit of Michael Jordan lore.

In April of 1986, Jordan set an NBA playoff record by scoring sixty-three points in an overtime loss to the Boston Celtics. In that game, he went to the foul line twenty-one times, and made nineteen of his free throws (a remarkable percentage). So despondent was he, though,

at missing a couple that the next morning, he was up at the crack of dawn and in the gym shooting baskets, a full three hours before his team was scheduled to practise. This after scoring sixty-three points and almost single-handedly beating what was then the best team in basketball! Crosby digested this anecdote for a moment, looked down at his smoothie, paused, looked back up, and laid this one on me— "I guess it's no coincidence that the people who are best at what they do just happen to work the hardest." That pearl of wisdom from a fourteen-year-old kid in the food court of a mall. I've never forgotten it.

From my most memorable moment to a personal favourite: In March of 2005, I took my dad to Rimouski to watch Crosby play a couple of games in his final year of junior hockey. After the game on Saturday afternoon, Crosby and his father met the two of us for dinner at the hotel restaurant. It was a great time, a chance for Crosby to let down his guard a bit and just kick back. No cameras, no microphones, no notepads—just some guys at a table laughing hard for two or three hours. The key point I'd like to make is that this was the first and only time my dad had ever met Crosby and had the chance to talk to him. And he wouldn't see him again for another two years....

By that time, Crosby was the NHL's biggest star with the Pittsburgh Penguins. I was assigned to work a Penguins-Canadiens game in Montreal and, as a Christmas gift for my dad, I arranged for him to accompany me and watch the game from the press box.

On the morning of the game, the Penguins went through a quick practice and then returned to their dressing room to speak to media members. There must have been fifty, maybe even sixty reporters around Crosby's locker. I walked in with my dad and we stood in the corner of the room just to watch what was going on. As we quietly observed the mayhem, there was a suddenly a sliver of light between two reporters, and through that sliver Crosby and I made fleeting eye

SIDNEY CROSBY

contact. At that moment, he excused himself from further questions, stood up, and weaved his way through the throng to where we were standing. Without hesitation, he extended his right hand to my dad and said, "Mr. Rainnie, it's good to see you again." For Crosby, this was a full twenty-two months and maybe a million people after the dinner in Rimouski, and yet he remembered. You could have knocked my dad over with a feather. That, my friends, is *duende*. The very definition.

TIMELINE

AUGUST 7, 1987

Born in Halifax, Nova Scotia (Hometown: Cole Harbour)
Crosby later chose his now famous number 87 based on his birthdate. Coincidentally, it also matched a contract he would later sign for $8.7 million.

1990

Age 2 1/2: Learned to skate.

1992

Age 5: Started school. Crosby was an "A" student throughout his education.

1993–94

Age 6: Played for the Novice Cole Harbour Red Wings and won his first trophy.

1994–95

Age 7: With the Novice Cole Harbour Red Wings, scored 34 goals and 14 assists in 52 games. Crosby also gave his first media interview with the *Daily News*.

1995–96

Age 8: Became a brother to little sister and future goaltender Taylor.

1996–97

Age 9: Played with the Atom AAA Cole Harbour Red Wings and won a provincial championship.

1997–98

Age 10: Scored more than 100 goals in a season with the Atom AAA Cole Harbour Red Wings, repeated as provincial champion, and won MVP and Top Scorer.

1998–99

Age 11: Played for the PeeWee AAA Cole Harbour Red Wings and won provincial and Atlantic championships. Crosby was named tournament All-Star at the Atlantics.

1999–2000

Age 12: With the PeeWee AAA Red Wings, scored more than 100 goals in the regular season. This team repeated as provincial and Atlantic champions, and Crosby was named MVP and Top Scorer at the Atlantics.

2000–01

Age 13: With the Bantam Cole Harbour Red Wings, Crosby won provincial and Atlantic championships and was Top Scorer and MVP in both tournaments.

2001–02

Age 14: With the Dartmouth Midget AAA Subways, Crosby scored more than 100 goals and led the team to the Air Canada Cup, where he became the youngest player to ever be named MVP. Also, he was featured for the first time on CBC's *Hockey Day in Canada*.

2002–03

Age 15: Attended Shattuck St. Mary's prep school in Minnesota and won a National Championship. Crosby also set a league scoring record of 72 goals and 162 points in 57 games. He played for Nova Scotia at the 2003 Canada Games as well, leading the tournament in

SIDNEY
CROSBY

scoring and receiving the Roland Michener award for leadership and excellence.

2003–04

Age 16: Drafted first overall by Rimouski of the QMJHL. He was named Player of the Year, Top Rookie, and Top Scorer—the only QMJHL player to ever receive all three awards in one season. He led the QMJHL in scoring with 54 goals and 81 assists in only 59 regular season games. He also became only the fifth sixteen-year-old to play for Canada at the World Junior Hockey Championship.

2004–05

Age 17: Played for Rimouski of the QMJHL and was named MVP, Top Scorer, Offensive Player of the Year, Top Pro Prospect, and Personality of the Year. He won gold with Canada at the World Junior Hockey Championship.

2005–06

Age 18: Drafted first overall by the Pittsburgh Penguins, he became the youngest player in NHL history to record 100 points in a season. Played for Canada at the World Hockey Championship and led the tournament in scoring with 8 goals and 8 assists in 9 games.

2006–07

Age 19: With Pittsburgh, he became the youngest player to be named captain. He was also the youngest to lead the NHL in scoring at 19 years and 244 days. Crosby was the youngest player in NHL history to have two consecutive 100-point seasons. He was named league MVP, Ted Lindsay Award-winner, recipient of the Lester B. Pearson Award (youngest ever), and Canada's Top Athlete. Crosby was the youngest player to start in an All-Star game and the youngest to be named to the year-end First All-Star Team.

2007-08

Age 20: Led the Penguins to an Atlantic Division title with 47 wins and 102 points. The Penguins defeated Ottawa in four games to advance to the second round of playoffs. In the NHL's first Winter Classic, Crosby scored the overtime winner in a snowstorm to beat Buffalo.

2008-09

Age 21: Surpassed 100 career goals, 200 assists, and 300 points. Crosby finished third in NHL scoring. The Penguins defeated the Red Wings in the Stanley Cup final and Crosby became the youngest captain in modern times to lead his team to a championship.

2009-10

Age 22: With 51 goals, won the Maurice "Rocket" Richard Trophy as the NHL's leading goal scorer. He tied for second in the NHL points race. At the Winter Olympics in Vancouver, he scored the gold-medal-winning goal in overtime against the United States.

2010-11

Age 23: Had a 25-game point-scoring streak. He suffered a concussion at the Winter Classic on January 1, 2011. He would play his last game of the season on January 5.

2011-12

Age 24: Missed the first 20 games of the season recovering from a concussion. Scored 37 points in the 22 games he played that season.

2012-13

Age 25: In a lock out–shortened season, won the Ted Lindsay Award and finished runner-up in league MVP voting. He also won the Bill Masterton Memorial Trophy for dedication and perseverance.

SIDNEY CROSBY

2013–14

Age 26: Played 80 games for the first time since 2010, finishing with a league-high 104 points. Crosby won his second Art Ross Trophy. He also won his second Hart Trophy as league MVP and his third Ted Lindsay Award as the players' choice for league's best player. Crosby was captain of the Olympic men's hockey team that won gold in Sochi, Russia.

2014–15

Age 27: Crosby scored his 300th goal and 800th career point. He finished third in league scoring. He was also captain of the Canadian team that won gold at the World Hockey Championship. With that achievement, he became a member of the Triple Gold Club (World Junior, World Hockey, Olympics), and the first to captain all three.

2015–16

Age 28: Scored his 900th career point and 600th career assist. He was named a finalist for league MVP. The Penguins won the Stanley Cup, and Crosby was named Playoff MVP.

2016–17

Age 29: Scored his 1,000th NHL point (the 11th youngest to do so), won his third Stanley Cup (second in a row) and again was named Playoff MVP.

2017

Age 30: Was named by the Nova Scotia Sport Hall of Fame as the greatest Nova Scotian athlete of all time.

15 FACTS ABOUT SIDNEY CROSBY

1 Crosby began playing hockey in his basement at age two and began skating at age two and a half.

2 Crosby's favourite player as a youngster was Detroit captain Steve Yzerman.

3 Sidney's father, Troy, was an excellent goalie who played for the Verdun Canadiens of the QMJHL.

4 Sidney Crosby was born on August 7, 1987. The 7th day of the 8th month, 1987. No wonder he chose #87 for his uniform.

5 Many hockey fans think that Crosby deliberately shot pucks at the family dryer. This is not the case. He shot pucks at a net in his basement and when he missed wide, it would hit the dryer. Suffice to say, even the best miss a lot!

6 At the age of fourteen, Crosby was profiled on CBC's *Hockey Day in Canada*.

7 As a fourteen-year old, Crosby led the Dartmouth Midget AAA Subways to a second-place place finish at the 2002 Air Canada Cup. He finished the tournament with 24 points in 7 games and was named tournament MVP.

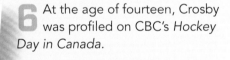

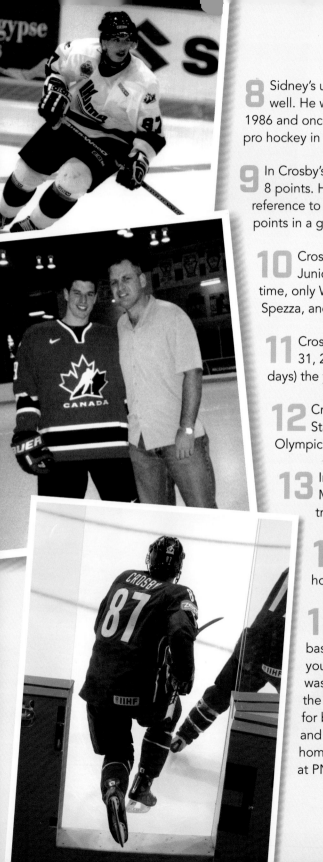

8 Sidney's uncle, Robert Forbes, was a tremendous player as well. He won an Allan Cup with the Corner Brook Royals in 1986 and once scored 62 goals and 121 points in a season of pro hockey in Europe.

9 In Crosby's first exhibition game with Rimouski, he recorded 8 points. His teammates nicknamed him "Darryl," in reference to Darryl Sittler, who once recorded a record 10 points in a game with the Toronto Maple Leafs.

10 Crosby played for Team Canada at the (2004) World Junior Hockey Championship as a 16 year old. At the time, only Wayne Gretzky, Mario Lemieux, Eric Lindros, Jason Spezza, and Jay Bouwmeester had previously done so.

11 Crosby was named Pittsburgh's team captain on May 31, 2007, making him (at 19 years, 9 months, and 24 days) the youngest team captain in NHL history.

12 Crosby is the only player ever to captain teams to Stanley Cup, World Cup, World Championship, and Olympic titles.

13 In 2017, Crosby became the first player since Mario Lemieux to win back-to-back Conn Smythe trophies as playoff MVP.

14 Crosby's first cousin, Forbes MacPherson, is the head coach of the UPEI Panthers men's hockey program.

15 Crosby was also a gifted baseball player as a youth. In 2010, he was invited to join the Pittsburgh Pirates for batting practice, and hit a 370-foot home run to right field at PNC Park.

HONOURABLE MENTIONS

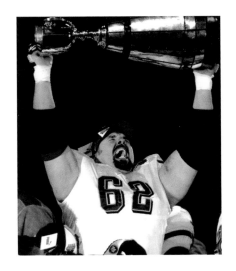

BRUCE BEATON

Born in Port Hood, Cape Breton, Bruce Beaton went on to have one of the most outstanding football careers of any Canadian player ever. A three-time All-Canadian at Acadia, Beaton later excelled with the Edmonton Eskimos, winning two Grey Cups and being named a member of the Eskimos' All-Century Team. Beaton was a three-time CFL All-Star and played for five teams in his thirteen-year CFL career.

TRACY CAMERON

Tracy Cameron of Shubenacadie was a three-time Female Athlete of the Year at Hants East Rural High School before attending Acadia to play basketball and earn her Education degree. At age twenty-five, she took up rowing. A week later, she told her coach she was going to the Olympics. Turns out she was right! A two-time World champion and the 2008 Olympic bronze medallist, Cameron is on the short list of finest rowers ever to come from Nova Scotia.

LYLE CARTER

Lyle Carter of Truro was a true two-sport star. He was an outstanding hockey goaltender who played a season in the NHL for the California Golden Seals. He was also one of the finest softball players in the history of Nova Scotia and was named an All-Canadian four times while playing for the Brookfield Elks. Former Softball Nova Scotia president Jack Gray believed that Carter was the finest softball player of the last quarter century.

JUSTINE COLLEY

Justine Colley of East Preston is one of the greatest players in the history of Canadian university basketball. During a remarkable five-year career with Saint Mary's, she was twice named national Player of the Year and was named All-Canadian four times. She is the all-time leading scorer in the history of CIS women's basketball. In 2013, she played a year for the Canadian senior national women's team and finished as the team's leading scorer.

MIKE FORGERON

Mike Forgeron of Main-a-Dieu, Cape Breton, was a long-time star member of Canada's national rowing team. He competed at two consecutive Summer Olympics and in 1992, was a member of the team that won the gold medal in the men's eights. In the 1996 Olympics, he competed in the men's double sculls, finishing seventh overall. Forgeron also won a gold

medal in a four-man boat at the 1994 Commonwealth Games, and a silver and bronze medal at the 1991 Pan American Games. He is a member of the Canadian Amateur Sport Hall of Fame.

ART HAFEY

Boxer Art Hafey of New Glasgow was once described by Angelo Dundee, the trainer of Muhammad Ali, as "the best little man I have ever seen." Throughout the 1970s, Hafey was widely considered to be one of the best featherweight fighters in the world. He fought 65 times as a pro, finishing with a record of 53 wins, 8 losses, and 4 draws. Among his victories was a 1973 knockout of the legendary Mexican fighter Ruben Olivares.

ANDREW HALEY

Andrew Haley of North Sydney overcame incredible odds to become one of the greatest swimmers in the province's history. As a young boy, he lost part of his right leg and his left lung to cancer. Undeterred, he began training to swim competitively at the age of fifteen and would soon become a Para World champion and world record holder in the 100-metre butterfly. Overall, he would win three World championship gold medals and five medals at Paralympic Games (one gold, four bronze). His personal motto: "Believing is the first step in doing."

HONOURABLE
MENTIONS

VINCE HORSMAN

Vince Horsman of Dartmouth grew up playing baseball in the Central Dartmouth Minor Baseball Association. It's a gargantuan jump from there to Major League Baseball, but Horsman made it. He pitched for three teams over his five seasons in the majors: the Toronto Blue Jays, Oakland A's, and Minnesota Twins. He posted a career win-loss record of 4-and-2, and racked up 61 strikeouts. He is one of only three Nova Scotians to have made it to the major leagues.

ANTE JAZIC

Ante Jazic of Bedford is without question the best soccer player ever to be developed in Nova Scotia. His resume includes sixteen years as a professional and thirty-six appearances for the Canadian national team. Jazic cracked the Nova Scotia Canada Games team (Under-20) as a seventeen-year-old in 1993, earned a bronze medal at the senior men's Nationals with Halifax King of Donair in 1994, and won a National Championship with the Dalhousie Tigers in 1995, where he was named conference Rookie of the Year and an All-Canadian. In 2006, he began a stint playing for the Los Angeles Galaxy of Major League Soccer, where his teammate was David Beckham.

KIRK JOHNSON

Kirk Johnson of North Preston is one of the finest boxers to ever come from the province. As an amateur, he posted a record of 76 wins and 7 losses, and represented Canada

at the 1992 Summer Olympics. His record as a professional was 37 wins, 2 losses, and 1 draw. He fought for the WBA heavyweight title in 2002, but was disqualified for repeated low blows. He was ranked among the top five heavyweights in the world for five straight years by *Ring Magazine*.

GLEN MURRAY

The pride of Bridgewater, Glen Murray was drafted in the first round of the 1991 NHL draft, eigh-

teenth overall, by the Boston Bruins. He played sixteen seasons in the NHL for the Boston Bruins, the Pittsburgh Penguins, and the Los Angeles Kings. He scored 337 goals and 651 points in just over 1,000 games played. He ranks fourth all-time in points scored by a Nova Scotia–born NHLer, trailing only Al MacInnis, Sidney Crosby, and Bobby Smith. Murray played in two NHL All-Star games (2003 and 2004) and was twice a member of Team Canada at the World Championship (winning gold in 2004).

GORDIE SMITH

Gordie Smith of Dartmouth is one of the finest golfers Nova Scotia has ever produced. He won the Nova Scotia Provincial Junior Championship twice and the Nova Scotia Amateur three times before attending the University of South Florida on a golf scholarship. As a professional, his career highlight came when he finished seventh in the 1988 Canadian Open ahead of greats

such as Jack Nicklaus and Greg Norman. Smith currently works as the general manager of the Ashburn Golf Club in Halifax.

LUCY SMITH

Lucy Smith of Bedford has won a combined nineteen National Championships in distance running, duathlon, and triathlon. She is a two-time World Duathlon Championship silver medallist and is one of Canada's most versatile endurance athletes with unparalleled results over a wide range of distances and disciplines. As a student at Dalhousie University in the late 1980s, she was two-time CIAU cross-country champion (1988 and 1989) and in each case was named Dal's Athlete of the Year.

MARJORIE TURNER-BAILEY

Marjorie Turner-Bailey of Lockeport was a star soccer and basketball player for her high school teams. She first gained provincial and Maritime recognition during the spring of 1964 when she astounded track and field followers with her sheer speed and strength at a Mount Allison University Invitation and the famed Acadia Relays. She finished with a first-place showing in the 100- and 200-yard dashes, the broad jump, and the shot put. During her career, she would go on to set four

Canadian track and field records and win medals at Pan Am and Commonwealth Games. She competed in the 1976 Montreal Olympics.

TYRONE WILLIAMS

Halifax's Tyrone Williams was a standout in basketball and football at Queen Elizabeth High School. He was a two-time All-Canadian football star at the University of Western Ontario. He was also MVP of the 1989 Vanier Cup, won by his Mustangs. One of his greatest achievements was winning two Super Bowl rings as a member of the Dallas Cowboys. He also won a Grey Cup ring as a member of the Toronto Argonauts. Williams is the only Canadian athlete to win the Vanier Cup, Grey Cup, and Super Bowl.

15 FACTS ABOUT THE NOVA SCOTIA SPORT HALL OF FAME

1 Former Halifax Mayor J. E. (Gee) Ahern initiated the idea for the Hall of Fame because he wanted to recognize Nova Scotia's role in the origins of hockey.

2 With the help of Earl Morton, Harry Butler, and Alex Nickerson, the Hall opened on November 3, 1964, in the Industrial Building in the Halifax Forum Complex.

3 The Hall of Fame's first Induction Night was held on September 20, 1980, hosted by Hall of Famer Pat Connolly.

4 The Hall of Fame reopened in its first permanent facility in 1983 at the Brewery Market on Lower Water Street, Halifax.

5 Bill Robinson was the Hall's first executive director/CEO (1983–2017). A star quarterback with the Saint Mary's Huskies, he won Vanier Cups with SMU and UWO, and a Grey Cup with the Ottawa Roughriders.

6 The Hall of Fame had locations in the World Trade and Convention Centre and the Centennial Building before moving to the Scotiabank Centre (formerly Halifax Metro Centre).

7 The Hall's current location opened September 16, 2006.

8 The Hall of Fame honours close to 550 inductees.

9 There are over 7,700 items in the museum collection, all accessible online at www.novamuse.ca.

10 Inductees are nominated by the public and selected via a rigorous process involving a panel and a committee.

11 The Hall of Fame's Future Hall of Famers education program reaches over 15,000 youth each year.

12 The education program is free and available to all schools across the province.

13 The Hall of Fame museum offers free admission year-round!

14 The Hall is lucky to be home to a large Sidney Crosby display including the famous Crosby family dryer.

15 You can find every inductee in the Nova Scotia Sport Hall of Fame, and much more information on the organization, by visiting www.nsshf.com.

JAMIE BONE

STEVE GILES

MY TOP 15

The Top 15 sparked debate, brought names from the past back into the spotlight, and had many people wondering how they might have judged things differently. Have the final word with your own list and rank the Top 15 greatest Nova Scotia athletes of all time below:

1. _____
2. _____
3. _____
4. _____
5. _____
6. _____
7. _____
8. _____
9. _____
10. _____
11. _____
12. _____
13. _____
14. _____
15. _____

COLLEEN JONES

AL MACINNIS (MIDDLE)

PHOTO CREDITS

All photos were contributed by the Nova Scotia Sport Hall of Fame or the subjects, except as follows:

Associated Press: p. 94 (photographer: Mark Humphrey), p. 102 (photographer: Jeffrey T. Barnes)

Atlantic Division CanoeKayak Canada: p. 25 (Alex Scott; Craig Spence)

Canada's Sports Hall of Fame: Front cover (Sam Langford; George Dixon), p. 66

The Canadian Press: Front Cover (Sidney Crosby, photographer: Ryan Remiorz), p. 9 (photographer: Ryan Remiorz), p. 19 (photographer: Mark Blinch), p. 21 (photographer: Nathan Denette), p. 23 (photographer: Ryan Remiorz), p. 72 (Brad Marchand, photographer: Nathan Denette), p. 99 (photographer: Ryan Remiorz), p. 108 (photographer: Jonathan Hayward), p. 115 (Glen Murray, photographer: Frank Gunn)

Gymnastics Canada: Front Cover (Ellie Black)

Halifax *Chronicle Herald*: Front Cover (Mark de Jonge), p. 7, p. 10, p. 16, p. 25 (Blayre Turnbull), p. 26, p. 29, p. 30 (Chelsey Gotell), p. 57 (Jenna Martin), p. 72 (Barry Patriquin), p. 114 (Kirk Johnson)

Halifax Mooseheads: p. 24 (Nathan MacKinnon)

Hockey Canada Images: p. 31 (Jillian Saulnier, photographer: Dave Holland)

Iowa State University: p. 25 (Lindell Wigginton)

Klaver, Andrew: Front Cover (Colleen Jones), p. 38 (Colleen Jones curling rink), p. 87, p. 88, p. 91, p. 122

MacKinnon, Bruce: p. 16

Manitoba Sports Hall of Fame: p. 12 (Robert Boucher)

Nova Scotia Archives: p. 49, p. 61, p. 67

Pearce, Nick: p. 57 (Geoff Harris), p. 58 (Adrienne Power), p. 79 (David Sharpe), p. 112 (Justine Colley)

St. Francis Xavier University: p. 78 (Eric Gillis)

University of Alabama: p. 24 (Nate Darling)

THANK YOUS

Thank you again to our charitable partner in this project, the Tim Horton Children's Foundation.

Another thank you to everyone on the Top 15 panel and committee, including the members of the public who cast their votes, for the enthusiasm that they brought to the Top 15 countdown.

Thank you to our team—the Hall of Fame staff, extended family of dedicated volunteers, and 2016 summer students Annalise Benoit and Kelsey Whynot— for assisting with the many steps of the Top 15 process and related projects. And thank you to the *Halifax Chronicle Herald* and CBC Nova Scotia for their coverage of the countdown.

A special thank you to the Crosby Family, the Johnny Miles Foundation, Cape Breton University, the *Chronicle Herald*, Pottersfield Press, and Ken Bagnall of Sport Centre Atlantic for their assistance with materials that appeared in this book.

The Top 15 logo design is the talented work of Kelly Devoe, and the chapter number design is thanks to Paul MacDougall of Sojourn Signs.

As always, we are grateful to the large community of inductees, local sports people, and sports organizations who supported this book and all other Hall of Fame projects.

Thank you to Nimbus Publishing for coaching us through this book on such a short timeline.

Last but not least, thank you to everyone who followed the countdown; who watched, listened, and read along as we revealed the Top 15; who shared their votes, likes, comments, and criticisms; who engaged and participated and picked up this book. There is no great sport moment without the fans, the audience, the spectators—so *thank you*.

SIDNEY CROSBY

ABOUT THE AUTHORS

LEAD AUTHOR

Katie Tanner is the museum and communications coordinator at the Nova Scotia Sport Hall of Fame. A graduate of Dalhousie University, Tanner (formerly Wooler) wrote articles for *Dal News* and *Dal Magazine* throughout her degree programs.

CONTRIBUTING AUTHORS

Bruce Rainnie is the president and CEO at the Nova Scotia Sport Hall of Fame. A long-time broadcaster and Olympic commentator with CBC, Rainnie is also the author of *Right Place, Right Time*, which reached number six on the *Globe and Mail* national bestseller list.

Joel Jacobson is a well-respected freelance journalist. A long-serving volunteer with the Nova Scotia Sport Hall of Fame, Jacobson chaired the Top 15 committee.

Steven Laffoley is an award-winning Canadian author of fiction and creative-nonfiction books. A freelance writer for nearly thirty years, Laffoley has also written essays for print and online magazines, newspapers, and radio.

A long-time journalist and communications specialist based in Halifax, Greg Guy is a senior communications officer at CBC. Guy has a keen interest in sports and has covered figure skating for most of his career, including three Olympic Winter Games in 2010, 2014, and, most recently, the 2018 Pyeongchang Games.

NOVA SCOTIA
Sport Hall of Fame

The Nova Scotia Sport Hall of Fame is a not-for-profit organization that honours, promotes and preserves Nova Scotia's rich sport history. The Hall of Fame offers a free-admission museum located in downtown Halifax, a free province-wide education program, and a collection of over 7,700 artifacts accessible to the public online. Originally conceived as a passion project of former Halifax mayor John "Gee" Ahern in 1964, the Hall of Fame was incorporated in 1983 and has continued to grow as new inductees are enshrined each year through a public nomination process. The Hall strives to share the stories of great athletic achievement in our province, with the goals of remembering sport's influence on our heritage, celebrating our communities, and inspiring future generations of Hall of Famers.

Please visit our website at www.nsshf.com to learn more.

OTHER BOOKS FOR SPORTS FANS FROM NIMBUS PUBLISHING

Play by Play: The Life and Times of Pat Connolly
Joel Jacobson
9781771080767

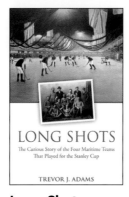

Long Shots
Trevor Adams
9781551099309

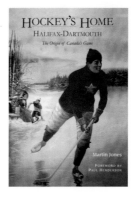

Hockey's Home
Martin Jones
9781551099484

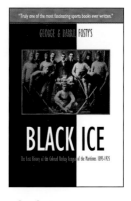

Black Ice
Darril Fosty &
George Fosty
9781551096957

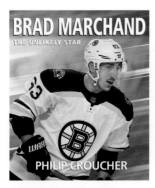

Brad Marchand
(coming Oct 2018)
Philip Croucher
9781771086851

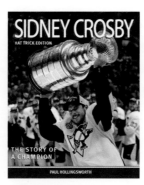

**Sidney Crosby
(Hat Trick edition)**
Paul Hollingsworth
9781771084277

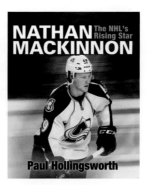

Nathan MacKinnon
Paul Hollingsworth
9781771083317

It's Not Just a Game
Eric Crookshank
9781551099590